PRAISE FOR
Awakening Osiris

"Normandi Ellis is a genius. Her years of study of the ancient Egyptian language, her deep understanding of the spiritual message of the ancient Egyptian texts, and her exceptional gifts as a poet combine to make *Awakening Osiris* the best and most beautiful interpretation ever offered of the ancient Egyptian Book of the Dead—which, of course, celebrates not death but life with all its joys and all its mysteries."

> —**GRAHAM HANCOCK,** bestselling author of
> *Fingerprints of the Gods and Visionary*

"I have read *Awakening Osiris* more than any other book—ever—in my extensive library. Normandi Ellis's interpretation of the Egyptian Book of the Dead is an utterly unique combination of scholarship and poetry. It presents this most important work of Western spirituality in a gorgeously accessible way. *Awakening Osiris* is a perennial, a classic in the combined realm of Egyptology, spirituality, and pure literary achievement."

> —**KATHLEEN MCGOWAN,** *New York Times*
> bestselling author of *The Expected One*

"*Awakening Osiris* is not only a translation and a book of Egyptian religion but also a spiritual work that will serve many pagans as a prayer book of sorts, a book of meditations—something not to be read and left on the shelf but to return to repeatedly."

> —**JUDIKA ILLES,** author of *Encyclopedia of*
> *Spirits*

"Anyone reading this work cannot help but be moved by it. It comes as close to an appreciation of the themes of the soul's journey portrayed in the Egyptian Book of the Dead as any modern interpretation has, and with a poetry unmatched anywhere in the literature thus far."

—*KMT: A Modern Journal of Ancient Egypt*

"*Awakening Osiris* has been my companion for the greater part of my life, always returning me to the wholesome, healthy, and holy. It makes sense of living and dying. Normandi Ellis's understanding of the many nuances of the Book of the Dead breathes life into the words, making ancient Egypt live again, while never losing touch with the present."

—**TAMRA LUCID**, author of *Making the Ordinary Extraordinary*

"Not a translation, a reinvention—in itself a great work of poetic art. From devoted study and long immersion in the writing of ancient Egypt arose this celebration of life and illumination of death, filled with beautiful appreciations of the details of love and living. Read *Awakening Osiris* to someone you love."

—**RONNIE PONTIAC**, author of American *Metaphysical Religion*

AWAKENING
OSIRIS

AWAKENING OSIRIS

THE SPIRITUAL KEYS TO THE
Egyptian Book of the Dead

NORMANDI ELLIS

NEW
PAGE

This edition first published in 2023 by New Page Books, an imprint of
Red Wheel/Weiser, LLC
With offices at:
65 Parker Street, Suite 7
Newburyport, MA 01950
www.redwheelweiser.com

Every effort has been made to trace copyright holders and to obtain their permission for the
use of copyright material. The publisher apologizes for any errors or omissions and would
be grateful if notified of any corrections that should be incorporated in future reprints or
editions of this book.

ISBN: 978-1-63748-010-6

Library of Congress Cataloging-in-Publication Data

Names: Ellis, Normandi, translator, writer of supplementary textual content.
Title: Awakening Osiris : the spiritual keys to the Egyptian book of the
    dead / Normandi Ellis.
Other titles: Book of the Dead. Selections. English (Ellis)
Description: Newburyport, MA : New Page, 2023. | Includes bibliographical
    references. | Summary: "The Egyptian Book of the Dead is one of the
    oldest and greatest classics of Western spirituality. Until now, the
    available translations have treated these writings as historical
    curiosities that have little relevance to our contemporary situations.
    This new version, made from the hieroglyphs, approaches the Book of the
    Dead as a profound spiritual text capable of speaking to us today. These
    writings suggest that the divine realm and the human realm are not
    altogether separate-they remind us that the natural world, and the
    substance of our lives, is fashioned from the stuff of the gods"—
    Provided by publisher.
Identifiers: LCCN 2022057694 | ISBN 9781637480106 (paperback) | ISBN
    9781633412811 (kindle edition)
Subjects: LCSH: Incantations, Egyptian. | Future life—Ancient Egyptian
    religion—Early works to 1800. | BISAC: BODY, MIND & SPIRIT / Afterlife
    & Reincarnation | BODY, MIND & SPIRIT / Ancient Mysteries &
    Controversial Knowledge
Classification: LCC PJ1555.E5 E44 2023 | DDC 299/.31—dc23/eng/20230125
LC record available at https://lccn.loc.gov/2022057694

Cover design by Sky Peck Design
Cover art by Javier Cruz Domínguez
Interior by Happenstance Type-O-Rama
Typeset in Adobe Caslon Pro, Albertus MT, Benguiat Pro ITC, and Optima LT Std

Printed in the United States of America
IBI
10 9 8 7 6 5 4 3 2 1

For Randy
who believed so, too.

Contents

Original Introduction   xiii

Concordance   xxiii

New Introduction   1

---

1   The Return   15

2   Greeting Ra   18

3   Greeting Osiris   21

4   The Speeches   24

5   Coming Forth by Day   29

6   The History of Creation   33

7   The Duel   40

8   Triumph over Darkness   45

9   Seven Houses in the Other World   53

10   Twenty-One Women   60

11   Triumph through the Cities   66

12   The Arrival   70

13   Giving a Mouth to Osiris   72

14   Opening the Mouth of Osiris   73

15   Giving Charms to Osiris   74

16   Remembering His Name   75

17   Giving a Heart to Osiris   76

18   Giving Breath to Osiris   77

19   Drinking Water   78

20   Water and Fire   79

21   Fish Stink   80

22 Not Letting His Heart Be Carried Off   81
23 Not Scattering His Bones   84
24 Not Dying a Second Time   85
25 Not Letting His Head Be Severed   86
26 Not Decaying in the Other World   87
27 Not Allowing a Man to Pass East   88
28 Not Losing His Mind   89
29 Coming Forth and Passing Through   91
30 Bringing Home His Soul   92
31 His Soul and His Shadow   93
32 Returning to See His Home   95
33 Ra Rising   96
34 Awakening Osiris   97
35 A Preponderance of Starry Beings   98
36 Adoration of Ra   100
37 A Messenger of Ra   105
38 In the Talons of the Hawk   106
39 Before Changing   108
40 Becoming the Swallow   109
41 Becoming the Falcon of Gold   111
42 Becoming the Hawk Divine   112
43 Becoming One of the Ancients   119
44 Becoming the Craftsman   122
45 Becoming the Child   124
46 Becoming the Lotus   127
47 Becoming the Snake   128
48 Becoming the Crocodile   129
49 Becoming the Heron   130
50 Becoming the Phoenix   132
51 Becoming a Light in the Darkness   134

52 The Apes of Dawn   137

53 The Heart of Carnelian   138

54 The Cloth of Life   139

55 The Knot of Isis   140

56 The Pillow of Hands   141

57 The Column of Gold   142

58 The Eye of God   143

59 Entering the House   145

60 Entering Truth   147

61 The Confession   153

62 The Bath   160

63 This Body of Light   164

64 The Family   166

65 A Field of Flowers   171

66 Hymn to Ra   173

67 Hymn to Osiris   175

68 Hymn to Hathor   176

Appendix   177

Bibliography   199

The Ages of Grace ... 107

The Heart of Catechism ... 128

The Crash of Time ... 130

The Knot of Ink ... 118

The Pillow of Earth ... 117

The Column of Salt ... 122

The Eye of God ... 138

Entering the House ... 135

Entering Hell ... 141

The Comission ... 133

The Bath ... 140

The Body of Light ... 144

The Family ... 146

Death of Flowers ... 185

Hymn to Ra ... 178

Hymn to Osiris ... 173

The Right to Harbor ... 178

Appendix ... 177

Bibliography ... 191

Original Introduction

AFTER I HAD BEEN AT work some years on this text, a fellow asked me why I bothered with a subject as dreary as the Book of the Dead. "I mean, isn't it morbid? All that fascination with the dead and the dying and decay? What can you possibly see in it?" His question is fairly common. People unfamiliar with the text maintain a notion that it is somehow ghoulish. It is not. It is one of the most beautiful celebrations of life that I have ever read.

Osiris, the god of the dead, is a green god, an image of the seed waiting in the dark to burst forth into renewal. His death and rebirth illuminated the path from darkness to light, from unconsciousness to enlightenment. In that light, I called this book *Awakening Osiris,* for I thought of it as a call to consciousness and spiritual awakening. We are all Osirises.

The Book of the Dead is a misnomer applied by historians to a text which the ancient Egyptians referred to as the Book of Coming Forth by Day. I much prefer the Egyptian title as it seems best to represent what the book implies. No definitive version of the Book of the Dead exists. Rather it is a compilation of funerary texts and religious hymns written by priests and copied by scribes during a period spanning approximately 3000 BCE to 300 AD. In it are included versions of several other texts, which are detailed below.

The Pyramid Texts, the most ancient body of literature known, were inscribed on the walls of pyramids and pharaonic tombs during the Fifth and Sixth Dynasties of the Old Kingdom (2464–2355 BCE). They were supplications to the gods and goddesses that a man might achieve unity with the deities in heaven. The Coffin Texts appeared in the early Middle Kingdom (2154–1845 BCE) and usually were written in ink directly on the coffins of the noblemen and women who composed the pharaoh's entourage. These "spells," as historians have called them (though the Egyptians called them "chapters"), were intended to assure a human's unity with the gods by preventing the ravages of the body in the neter-world. Other chapters in the Book of the Dead owe their origin to such works as The Book of What Is in Tuat (the neterworld), the Book of Gates, the Book of Transformations, the Litany of the Sun, and various other hymns to the gods and goddesses.

The order of the chapters was diverse. In fact, the literature was in no manner a book as we perceive it with a beginning, middle and end. It was, instead, a compilation of chapters, each chapter unique unto itself and sometimes particular to the requirements of the pharaoh for whom it was written.

The Book of the Dead went through various revisions, additions and deletions in its history according to whatever theological doctrine was current to a particular region at that particular time. The priests of Amun, for example, assumed for their god the characteristics of Ra. By the Saite Recension (300 BCE) Osiris himself had over 150 forms, characteristics of other deities which he had assumed. The evil power of darkness, Set himself, possessed many names and many other entities of darkness and destruction followed in his train.

These subtle changes in theocracy took place at the priests' instigations in an effort to prevent a community from taking issue with a change in worship. Religious history is full of similar incorporations, such as the Hebrew practice of circumcision learned from the ancient Egyptians, or the Christian celebration of Christ's birth as coincidental with the ancient celebration of the winter solstice. Any drastic changes in the theocracy would have created upheaval. For example, when Akhenaton insisted on the divinity of the one god, he overthrew all at once the local gods. His heretical beliefs won him no favors with either his subjects or the priests. After his reign the ancient Egyptians effaced his name from the monuments—a powerful form of ancient curse—and they immediately returned to their worship of the beatific multitudes.

It is evident, then, that after 4,000 years of development and change, the authorship of The Book of the Dead cannot be ascribed to one particular individual. In fact, it cannot be ascribed to any individuals. The scribes for the most part simply copied what the priests instructed them to copy. Who these scribes and priests were is lost to history.

Ownership of the words was theologically impossible anyway, as the texts were divinely inspired. Certain chapters of the work are said to have been written by Thoth himself "with his own fingers." To Thoth—"lord of divine speech," "lord of Maat (truth)" and "lord of divine books"— was attributed the authorship of 42 sacred texts collectively entitled "The Books of Thoth." These dealt with sacred laws, astronomy, medicine, the history of the world and the work of priests. Some historians, such as H. Brugsch, believe that the original inscriptions of some of these chapters appear on the walls of the Temple of Horus at Edfu, but the claim is unsubstantiated and probably will remain so. The Greeks identified Thoth with Hermes, and he may have been the "Thrice Greatest Hermes" of which the mystics speak. The contents of the texts were, so we are told, not tampered with by the scribes, although the priests and pharaohs made revisions and personal supplications.

By and large, the hieroglyphs which we associate with the ancient Egyptians were the "holy writings" of the priests used during the Old Kingdom. Only priests were literate then, but by the Middle Kingdom, the business community and the scribes began to write in a cursive form of hieroglyphs called hieratics, which in the later dynasties was transmuted into the language of demotics. Near the end of the New Kingdom era, by and large, the use of hieroglyphs disappeared, for even the priests no longer knew the original meaning of the glyphs.

During the switch from hieroglyphics to hieratics, the alphabet lost its graphic or symbolic appeal. It was not necessary, for example, to illustrate the work of The Pyramid Texts as the hieroglyphics themselves were pictorial. It was necessary, however, to illustrate a papyrus written in hieratic as, by that time, the characters had become more or less abstractions implying sounds only; and since the general populace could not read, the people needed a picture to guide them in understanding the implications of each chapter.

By the end of the Middle Kingdom the scribes who worked on the texts were many, and the papyrus scrolls were often mass produced for the common people. One scribe may have worked only on illustrating the text with vignettes before he passed along the text to the next scribe who inscribed the hieroglyphs for a particular chapter. As a result the writing in the texts is often cramped, occasionally illegible or sometimes contains blank areas where too much space was left by the illustrator. In addition, blank spaces were left in the text where the name of a man could be inserted after the papyrus was purchased. This mass production resulted in several mistakes in various texts, but the circumstances of production make these understandable.

What has survived of Egyptian literature is primarily texts of religious rites, hymns, love songs and work songs. (Some notable exceptions include The Tale of Two Brothers and the wonderful Dialogue between a Man Weary of Life and His Soul, which was beautifully translated by Bika Reed as *The Rebel in the Soul.*) Little poetry or fiction as we tend to think of it has survived. Although rhyme was not a consideration, certain poetic elements appear such as repetition, alliteration, assonance, allusion, imagery and parallel structure. These were enhanced by a strong meter and rhythm in the work. The Egyptians loved puns of all types and even their religious texts are full of humor. Many times they intertwined sacred and profane images. It is interesting to note the many uses of the anagram; that is, how one word expressing a particular idea may have been spelled backward to represent an opposing idea. For example, kha indicates a corpse, while akh indicates a thing radiant or spiritual.

Language was of primary importance; in essence it cast a type of spell. The ancient Egyptians felt that if words could be uttered precisely, in proper sequence and with proper intonation, those words could produce magical effects. The Fourth Gospel begins: "In the beginning was the Word." In like manner the Egyptian History of the Creation of the Gods and the World begins with the words of Ptah, sometimes merged with the evening sun god Atum. (Both gods have similar stories of speaking the world into being, by opening their lips and having light spring forth from the darkness; yet each god derives from a different city in the delta.):

I am he who came into being, being what I created—
the creator of the creations . . .
After I created my own becoming,
I created many things
that came forth from my mouth.
(Nuk pu kheper em Kheperå
kheper-nå kheper kheperu
kheper kheperu
neb em-khet kheper-å asht kheperu
em per em re-å)

In addition, re-å for the mouth and Re (or Ra) for the sun god are similar. The implication, then, may be that Atum opened his mouth and light burst forth. The lions of yesterday and today (time) were symbols of Ra and these were called re-re, or the sound of lions roaring. One begins to see how intricately linked are the sound, symbol, myth and meaning. Language, then, resonates on and on in an intricate spiral of meanings, one word or association leading to the next.

What is most unfortunate is that we are uncertain as to exactly how the language was pronounced. The hieroglyphs were an alphabet of consonants, homophones and ideograms. The vowel sounds, or those breathy vocalizations, were sacred and therefore unwritten or secret. As a result the pronunciation of the text (and in Egyptian terms its precise meaning) is lost to us now.

An abundance of gods and goddesses appear in the text. Some are mentioned briefly and others are mentioned over and over again. Often times the minor names represent local deities incorporated into the greater gods and goddesses. Still, there seems to have been a time early in the development of the religion where the gods were one. The text often refers to one god—sometimes Atum, sometimes Ptah, sometimes Ra, depending on the interpretations of the priests that have been passed down to us. This one god was the creator of himself and all things therein. His name is secret and hidden. All the other gods and goddesses issue forth from him. One might think, then, of the other multitudes as aspects of the one god.

The Egyptian word which we have translated as "god" is neter, as in the "neterworld." But the word god, though common to us, seems imprecise when applied to Egyptian religion. Neter refers primarily to a spiritual essence, or principle. Our word "nature" may derive from it through the Latin. The multitudes of neteru, then, represent the multitudinous natures of supreme being. As John West pointed out in his book, *Serpent in the Sky*, the various religious centers of Heliopolis, Memphis, Hermopolis and Thebes, for example, were not advocating different gods. They were advocating differing aspects of god.

From the mouth of one supreme god came what is known as the Great Ennead, or the nine gods (neteru) of the one. In Heliopolis these were: Atum, Shu, Tefnut, Geb, Nut, Osiris, Isis, Set and Nephthys. In Memphis, Ptah and Hathor play major roles. In Hermopolis, Thoth is elevated. Ra, as a principle of light, eternity, power and rebirth, attained prominence nearly everywhere.

Atum and Ptah are aspects of one neter. Atum may be thought of as the primordial act, the first creation, pure essence and spirit. Ptah is Atum come to earth: the same principle of spirit, but in this instance he is the manifestation of the act of creating matter. The remaining neteru of the great ennead are paired male and female. They are unified dual natures. Shu and Tefnut are the twin children of Ra, the breath of light one might say. He personifies the dry air and she the mist. Geb, the father, is earth; Nut, the mother, is sky.

From the belly of Nut sprang the other gods and goddesses and Horus, the twice-born. Horus was born once of heaven through Nut and once of earth through his mother, Isis. He represents both the divine and mortal aspects of man, and his presence in the Book of the Dead is always as that of the great spiritual warrior. As the avenger of his father's death, he best represents the strength of the individual in his necessary battle against the power of darkness.

Osiris and Isis represent the dawning of the human world. All the descendants of the world are children of their son, Horus. My chapters "The History of Creation" and "The Duel" explain these myths in more detail. For a more in-depth look at all the gods and goddesses, I recommend E.A. Wallis Budge's two-volume set, *The Gods of the Egyptians*. Suffice it to say here that Osiris was murdered "twice." First, his brother drowned him and sailed him in a wooden jeweled coffin far from Egypt. Isis retrieved him and brought him home, then he was hacked into fourteen pieces by his envious brother Set. According to Plutarch, Isis, the wife of Osiris, gathered the severed parts of her husband to facilitate his unification in the afterlife. Osiris became neither a god of heaven nor of earth, but a god of the nebulous world between. His importance in The Book of the Dead as judge in the neterworld is primary. All those who died after him called themselves an Osiris, for they wanted to be like him—a god who rose from death. Osiris is the principle of regeneration as Set is the principle of destruction. In psychological terms Osiris represents the re-collecting of the diverse aspects of oneself into a unified whole.

As Horus embodies the masculine energy of the spiritual warrior, Hathor embodies the feminine beauty of nature. She is the jubilant celebration of life with feasts and song, love and dance. Isis serves as an example of the nurturing aspect of wife and mother, as well as the emblem of magical wisdom. Her sister, Nephthys, represents sorrow, but also intuition.

In researching this text, I perceived certain etymological resonances which indicated, to me at least, that the ancient Egyptian culture and language are not as obscure as we moderns tend to believe. For example,

I found common roots between the Egyptian language and certain words in the English language which are derived from Latin and Greek. As an example I offer the following connections between Egyptian and English:

armen/arm
heku (magic utterance)/hex
neb (spiraling force of the universe)/nebulous
Satis (goddess of the flood, or meaning enough)/satisfy
aor (magic light)/aura.

According to Egyptian theology, the structure of a human being is not limited to only the mortal shell and spiritual self, but is a complex and interconnected structure where the physical body, spiritual body, mental and emotional states play one off the other. The physical body, the corpse, or that which corrupts after death is the khat. It is easy enough to define. Where trouble often arises is in defining the various spiritual aspects which are loosely attributed to what we think of as the soul.

The sekhem is, I believe, the mental form that a spiritual being assumes as part of willing itself into being. It exists in heaven and is more or less that power which one possesses to assume incarnation. In addition, a person's "ren," or name, is powerful and holy. To blot a person's name from history, to forget them, was to effectively destroy them.

The åb is the heart, the seat of knowledge, wisdom and understanding; it is the link between the physical body and the spiritual body. In contrast, the khu has been called the divine intelligence and is described as that which is radiant or shining. Åb represents what one may come to know of the world and oneself in silent meditation. Khu represents more or less the inspiration, the message of the gods.

E.A. Wallis Budge describes the ka as the ethereal double, but the term has lacked a more definitive translation for many years and is often confused with the other spiritual aspects. Ka has at times been thought of as one's higher self, the astral body. The ba was loosely defined as the soul, or that which was noble and sublime. Isha Schwaller de Lubicz explains these two aspects in this way: the ka is personal, the ba is universal. The ka on the other hand is creative and gives rise to other essences, while the ba is fixed.

One of the main symbols of the spiritual journey is the road bordered by flowers which represents the way of the heart. On this road, the dead walk into heaven, and by this same path one makes a journey toward self-transformation. It may be equivalent to the Buddhist notion of the Tao. For further clarification of Egyptian spirituality, I recommend reading John West's *Serpent in the Sky* and several books by R.A. Schwaller de Lubicz and his wife, Isha, including *Opening of the Way, Symbol and the Symbolic, Nature Word* and *The Temple in Man.*

I have mentioned various aspects of the Egyptian culture and The Book of the Dead to serve as an introduction to the text I offer here. At the time I wrote this book in 1981–1988, I was neither a historian nor a theologian. I am now, having followed my life's passion for many years, finally receiving a doctorate of divinity in comparative religions at age 68. As my friend the Kabbalist Samuel Avital told me once: "I am not simply a human being. I am a human becoming." The work which follows has been for me a process of transformation. I offer it as a record of my own study of the text and illumination by it. I have tried to remain true to the intent of the original, to illuminate the insights which the hieroglyphs offered, and to revive the sense of literature and song which seemed to me to have been lost in any strictly literal translation.

I hesitate even to call this a translation. It is a meditation. Certainly the writing of it was a transformation. I encourage anyone interested in the subject to read the work in the original, if possible, along with a good "strict" translation. I relied on the Budge version of The Papyrus of Ani. As he says, it is one of the most complete texts of the Book of the Dead, but the implication is, of course, that even that papyrus is not complete. As I read I found references to chapters which should have been included, but were not. I included them, therefore, using the Egyptian language of myth and the English words of the imagination. I inserted a few I thought should be there.* For those interested in comparing my versions with the hieroglyphs, I've included a concordance at the end of this introduction.

I took Pound at his word and tried to "make it new." I wanted to once again offer it up as a celebration of the beauty and terror of life. The awe of awakening unto a new day, or perhaps a new self. The wisdom of the ancients seems eternal, yet each of us are affecting our changes. The work of a lifetime is the process of returning to light and life. So it seemed right to blow a little dust off the old Egyptian book and let it shine anew in a more modem era.

I'd like to extend my thanks to the many kind souls who've helped me in the writing of this work, especially to Randy Schroth, for his attention to the details and nuances of the text and for his emotional support, and Alaina, my daughter, for teaching me the things I'd forgotten. I'd also like to thank Sidney Goldfarb for suggesting the project in the first place, Robert Kelly for listening, Donald Hughes for championing me, Robert Steiner for his comments, Wendell Berry and Richard Taylor for inspiring me, Tom Frick and David Fideler for encouraging me, Jessie Page for asking the right questions, and not least my parents for proofing, cooking, cleaning, watching my child and holding back the flood while I finished this work.

—NORMANDI ELLIS

---

* "Fish Stink," "Becoming the Child," and "The Cloth of Life" are mine.

Concordance

On Using the Concordance

Readers often ask where I found the hieroglyphs I translated. I pulled them from the Book of the Dead published by E.A. Wallis Budge. He used the rather lengthy Papyrus of Ani, a New Kingdom scribe, circa 1275 to 1250 BCE. The Ani papyrus was written in hieratic script; however, when Sir Wallis Budge published his book, he inserted the appropriate hieroglyphs above his translations. That made it I easier for me to work with than the hieratic. I am a visual person, and the hieroglyphs held a stronger energy than the simple word-for-word meanings that Budge assigned them.

While most of the chapters I translated are derived from the papyrus of Ani, a few of the chapters derived from a similar hieroglyphic text found in the papyri of Hunefer, Nebseni, and Nekhet, written during the same time period. Some of the chapters were New Kingdom versions of what were originally Old Kingdom Pyramid Texts and Middle Kingdom Coffin Texts, which were found on the tomb walls and coffins, respectively. Discovering all of this information a bit at a time allowed me to experience a kind of exhilaration at wending my way through the antiquated versions of the earlier texts, a kind of Indiana Jones thrill, if you will. I wanted to honor the work of all the scribes of whatever era who lent their talents to the books of the afterlife, and so I incorporated their work and vision as best I could.

What this means is that my work is a compilation of texts derived from many papyri. I cannot say this hieroglyph comes from that line of text. Even in the ancient world, no sanctioned version of the Book of the Dead exists; in fact, they were not a book at all but a collection of scripts, prayers, affirmations, and "spells." These were living documents—viable and variable; and the words and inflections could change over the years, according to an individual's spiritual proclivities. Certain chapters were intended to be part of every person's afterlife story, but even these were often unique. In many cases, the older versions of the books, repeated for over two thousand years, are a holy script, said to have been written originally by Thoth (Djheuty) with his own fingers. The most important chapters in the book were the Confessions and Weighing of the Heart, Opening the Mouth, and so on. One could personalize the adorations, the transformations, the healing sections.

Ani's book is considered the largest book of the afterlife ever found; it is on papyrus of approximately seventy feet or more in length. It was so voluminous that for the British Museum to display it, it had to be cut into lengths and hung on the walls. The various pages were attached to each other with a kind of natural glue; when completed, the pages were rolled into a single scroll. Ani, the author of this version, was a master teacher of scribes in training, living near the Valley of the Kings. Many of the chapters in his book were written by his students. We can tell this because there are many different handwriting styles—some more beautiful than others. Also, a couple of the chapters appear twice, perhaps as practice scripts by two different student scribes.

The text on the papyri were usually inscribed by one scribe and illustrated by another. The illustrations were not used in older texts, but they became necessary when the common people also wanted a book for their afterlife services and could not read the hieroglyphs or hieratic. Thus, the illustrations point to the meaning of the text for the benefit of the owner.

From what we can tell, there were approximately 192 different texts to choose from. In general, most of the chapters in *Awakening Osiris* derive from the Saite Recension texts, written around the 25th and 26th dynasties. In general, the following chapters from the Saite Recension run this way:

Chapters 1–16 concern the deceased entering the duat (underworld) and regaining the use of movement and speech.

Chapters 17–63 explore the origins of the cosmos, the world, and the gods. It offers a view of the roads and maps through the underworld, teaching the deceased the words and prayers that show how to live again. In this case, one learns to rise again as the morning sun.

Chapters 64–129 allow the soul to travel through the night sky on a solar barge. Prepared for one's meeting with Osiris in the underworld, one is given the power to speak and make statements of innocence from sin (a negative confession) as one's heart is weighed in the balance on the scales of Ma'at.

Chapters 130–189 align the deceased with the adored gods and goddesses. Given protective amulets and foods, the deceased can take on the cosmic powers of the divine.

The appearance of the chapters in *Awakening Osiris,* as in any other book of the afterlife, is a bit random. It is less important for the chapters to appear in narrative sequence, rather more important that they appear in the collection at all. I arranged the book according to how each individual piece resonated with the chapter before and after. I treated them, more or less, as a poem in and of itself, and was more concerned with poetic resonance than with whether they followed the fashion of the Saite Rescension.

Book Title	Papyrus Title	Chapter	Papyrus of
The Return	Adoration of Ra when he rises in the eastern horizon of heaven.	XV	Ani
Greeting Ra	Adoration of Ra by the by the royal scribe, captain of soldiers, Nekhet.	XV	Nekhet
Greeting Osiris	Adoration of Osiris, Unnefer, great god within Abydos.	XV	Nebseni
The Speeches	The chapter of not letting the heart of Osiris Ani be driven away from him in Neterkhert.	XXX	Ani

Book Title	Papyrus Title	Chapter	Papyrus of
Coming Forth by Day	Here begin the chapters of coming forth by day and of the songs of praise and of glorifying and of coming forth from and of going into the glorious Neterkhert in the beautiful Amenta; to be said on the day of the burial; going in after coming forth.	I	Ani
The History of Creation	Here begin the praises and glorifyings of coming out from and of going into the glorious Neterkhert in the beautiful Amenta, of coming forth by day in all the transformations which please him, of playing at senet and of setting in the sekh hall, and of coming forth as a living soul.	XVII	Ani
The Duel	(Same title)	XVII	Nebseni
Triumph over Darkness	(Same title)	XVII	Ani and Nebseni
Seven Houses in the Other World	The chapter to be said when Ani comes to the first arit.	CXLVII	Ani
Twenty-One Women	The chapter of renewing the pylons in the House of Osiris which is in the Sekhet-Aanru.	CXLVI	Ani
Triumph through the Cities	(Untitled)	XVIII	Ani
The Arrival	(Untitled)	XVIII	Nebseni

Book Title	Papyrus Title	Chapter	Papyrus of
Giving a Mouth to Osiris	The chapter of giving a mouth to Osiris Ani, the scribe and teller of the holy offerings of all the gods.	XXII	Ani
Opening the Mouth of Osiris	The chapter of opening the mouth of Osiris, the scribe, Ani.	XXIII	Ani
Giving Charms to Osiris	The chapter of bringing charms unto Osiris Ani in Neterkhert.	XXIV	Ani
Remembering His Name	The chapter of causing the deceased to remember his name in Neterkhert.	XXV	Nebseni
Giving a Heart to Osiris	The chapter of giving a heart unto Osiris Ani in Neterkhert.	XXVI	Ani
Giving Breath to Osiris	The chapter of giving breath in Neterkhert.	LIV	Ani
	Another chapter of giving breath.	LV	Nebseni
	Chapter of sniffing the air upon earth.	LVI	Nebseni
	The chapter of breathing the air and of having power over the water in Neterkhert.	LVIII	Ani
	The chapter of breathing the air and of having power over the water in Neterkhert.	LIX	Ani
Drinking Water	The chapter of drinking water in the Underworld	LXI	Nebseni
Water and Fire	The chapter of drinking and of not being burned in the fire.	LXIIIa	Nebseni

Book Title	Papyrus Title	Chapter	Papyrus of
	The chapter of not being scalded with water.	LXIIIb	Nebseni
Not Letting His Heart Be Carried Off	Not driving away his heart.	XXXb	Ani
	The chapter of not letting the heart of a man be taken away from him in Neterkhert.	XXVII	Ani
	Not letting his heart be carried away.	XXVIII	Nebseni
	The chapter of not letting the heart of Osiris Ani be driven away from him in Neterkhert.	XXIXa	Ani
	Not letting his heart be repulsed.	XXXb	Nebseni
Not Scattering His Bones	Repulsing the slaughterer in Sutenhenen.	XL	Ani
	(Untitled)	XLII	Ani
	The chapter of not entering into the divine block.	L	Ani
Not Dying a Second Time	The chapter of not dying a second time in Neterkhert.	XLIV	Ani
	The chapter of not dying a second time.	CLXXV	Ani
Not Letting His Head Be Severed	The chapter of not letting the head of a man be cut off from him in Neterkhert.	XLIII	Ani
Not Decaying in the Other World	The chapter of not suffering corruption in Neterkhert.	XLV	Ani

Book Title	Papyrus Title	Chapter	Papyrus of
	The chapter of not perishing and of becoming alive in Neterkhert.	XLVI	Ani
Not Allowing a Man to Pass East	The chapter of not letting a man pass over to the east in Neterkhert.	XCIII	Ani
	Another chapter	XCIIIa	Ani
Not Losing His Mind	The chapter of not letting the soul of a man be taken away from him in Neterkhert.	LXI	Ani
	The chapter of not letting the soul of a man be captive in Neterkhert.	XCI	Ani
Coming Forth and Passing Through	Chapter of coming forth by day and of living after death.	II	Ani
	Chapter of passing through Amenta and of coming forth by day.	VI	Ani
	Chapter of coming forth by day, having passed through the tomb.	IX	Ani
Bringing Home His Soul	The chapter of causing the soul to be united to its body in Neterkhert.	LXXIX	Ani
His Soul and His Shadow	The chapter of opening the tomb to the soul and the shadow, of coming forth by day and of getting power over the legs.	XCII	Ani
Returning to See His Home	The chapter of walking with the legs and of coming forth upon the earth.	LXXIV	Ani

Book Title	Papyrus Title	Chapter	Papyrus of
	The chapter of making a man to return to see again his home upon earth.	CXXXII	Ani
Ra Rising	A hymn of praise to Ra when he rises in the eastern sky.	XV_1	Ani
Awakening Osiris	Another chapter of one who comes forth by day against his foes in Neterkhert.	XLVIII	Ani
A Preponderance of Starry Beings	A hymn of praise to Osiris Unnefer, the great god in Abydos.	XV_2	Ani
Adoration of Ra	A hymn of praise to Ra when he rises in the eastern sky and when he sets in the land of life.	XV_3	Ani
A Messenger of Ra	(No title. This is a rubric only.)	XVI	Ani
In the Talons of the Hawk	A hymn of praise to Ra on the day of the month wherein he sails in the boat.	CXXXIV	Ani
Before Changing	A chapter to be said on the day of the month.	CXXXIII	Ani
Becoming the Swallow	The chapter of changing into a swallow.	LXXXVI	Ani
Becoming the Falcon of Gold	The chapter of changing into the golden hawk.	LXXVII	Ani
Becoming the Hawk Divine	The chapter of changing into a divine hawk.	LXXVIII	Ani

Book Title	Papyrus Title	Chapter	Papyrus of
Becoming One of the Ancients	The chapter of changing into the soul of Atum.	LXXXV	Ani
Becoming the Craftsman	The chapter of changing into Ptah.	LXXXII	Ani
Becoming the Lotus	The chapter of changing into the lotus.	LXXXI	Ani
Becoming the Snake	The chapter of changing into Seta.	LXXXVII	Ani
Becoming the Crocodile	The chapter of changing into a crocodile.	LXXXVIII	Ani
Becoming the Heron	The chapter of changing into a heron.	LXXXIV	Ani
Becoming the Phoenix	The chapter of changing into a bennu bird.	LXXXIII	Ani
Becoming a Light in the Darkness	The chapter of changing into the god who gives light in the darkness.	LXXX	Ani
The Apes of Dawn	(Rubric.)	CXXVI	Ani
The Heart of Carnelian	The chapter of a heart of carnelian.	XXIXb	Ani
The Knot of Isis	The chapter of a buckle of carnelian.	CLVI	Ani
The Pillow of Hands	The chapter of the pillow which is placed under the head.	CLXVI	Ani
The Column of Gold	The chapter of a tet of gold.	CLV	Ani

Book Title	Papyrus Title	Chapter	Papyrus of
The Eye of God	(Untitled)	XLII	Ani
Entering the House	The chapter of going unto the divine chiefs of Osiris.	CXXIV	Ani
Entering Truth	The chapter of entering into the hall of double right and truth; a hymn of praise to Osiris.	CXXV	Ani
	The following shall be said by a man when he comes unto the hall of double right and truth, wherein he is purged of all the sins which he has done and wherein he sees the faces of all the gods.	CXXV	Nebseni
The Confession	(Same title as Entering Truth—Ani version.)	CXXV	Ani
The Bath	(Same title as Entering Truth—Nebseni version.)	CXXV	Nebseni
This Body of Light	(Untitled)	XLII	Ani
The Family	(Untitled)	CLI	Ani
A Field of Flowers	Here begins the chapters of the Sekhet-hetepu and the chapters of coming forth by day and of going into and coming out from Neter-khert and arriving in the Sekhet-Aanru and of being in peace in the great city wherein are fresh breezes.	CX	Ani
Hymn to Ra	(Untitled)	CXLVIII	Ani

Book Title	Papyrus Title	Chapter	Papyrus of
Hymn to Osiris	A hymn of praise to Osiris, the dweller in Amenta, Unnefer within Abydos.	CLXXXVI	Ani
Hymn to Hathor	A hymn of praise to Hathor.	CLXXXV	Ani

New Introduction

READERS OFTEN ASK HOW I became interested in ancient Egypt, but I've come to think of the question as how did ancient Egypt become interested in me? After nearly forty years, I'm still not sure why this text called me to it. Certainly, though, there are no accidents. And if ever there was a text that held the record for longevity of being a book of spiritual wisdom, it would be the Book of the Dead, papyrus of Ani. It seems to have emerged full blown from the minds and hearts of masters at least as far back as four thousand years ago.

Before I published *Awakening Osiris* in 1988, I had never been to Egypt; but I felt it in my bones. As a pubescent child, I climbed into drainage tunnels in my neighborhood to write and illustrate poetry on the concrete walls. Even as a child I must have known in my core something about being a scribe in the narrow, darkened tomb corridors of Egypt's Valley of the Kings and Valley of the Queens. Fascinated by the mystical and poetic as a young adult, I read and reread the works of Dion Fortune and others.

One day, having graduated from university, living in my hometown, and wondering what to do with myself, I sat on the limestone wall outside the Old Capitol on Broadway when I ran into Robert, a handsome fellow from my old neighborhood who was a year older than me. The storm water tunnel, previously mentioned, had been on the property at the edge of the woods where his parents had built their house. Even having grown up in the same neighborhood and attending the same high school, we were still basically strangers to each other.

We sat on a wall, talking these many years later as if we were old friends. As it turned out, we had a lot in common. He was a writer, an outsider, and a mystic at heart. Robert described how, after he had been drafted to serve in the Vietnam War, his father, a local doctor, managed

1

to get him enlisted as a medic rather than as a front-line soldier. Soon after, he was contacted by a man from a Rosicrucian lodge somewhere in Ohio.

"I understand," the man said, "that you are going to be a medic in the war. I am here to teach you what you need to know to assist souls in transition."

So, Robert studied for a time with this man, then continued to study Rosicrucianism for years after. The day that I met Robert again, several years after his return from Vietnam, we wound up discussing metaphysical things in general.

He asked, "Have you ever read The Egyptian Book of the Dead?"

"No."

"You should read it." Convinced that I should get my hands on the book as soon as possible, he walked me across the street to Poor Richard's Bookstore. We stood in front of the shelf for a few minutes and then he pulled down a volume, saying, "Here it is. Buy it."

So, I bought it. Wallis Budge's *Egyptian Book of the Dead, Papyrus of Ani* is the book most people are familiar with. It contained the hieroglyphs with Budge's translation work below.

Robert had to go, but he showed up later that night at my house with a cardboard box full of books, a whole bunch of esoteric reading. He said, "I just found out I have to move out of my apartment and leave for my work tomorrow, so I'm taking everything to my parents' house—except these books, which I really don't want them to know I have. Now, I'm going to leave them with you to keep."

I said, "Okay, what are they?"

"They're all my Rosicrucian notebooks, all the teachings. You're really not supposed to show them around, but you might find these interesting, if you take a walk through them."

I said, "Okay."

He took off, and the long and short of it is I never saw him again.

Several months later, I moved to Boulder, Colorado. Somehow, during a spontaneous, mad move west, I found a mysterious spiritual home, a deep sense of belonging to a place I'd never been. It was the glory of those massive mountains rising up out of the plain, turning orange in the sunrise against an infinite blue sky. It felt holy and wholly familiar. I arrived with less than $300 in my boot and Robert's books, which I'd taken with me, believing that when he returned, he would ask my mother where I was, and I'd send his books back to him. But I didn't hear from him.

A year went by. I got a job and established residency. While visiting my family in Kentucky, I opened the newspaper to find an article saying that Robert had been missing for months, and finally his body had been found in Tennessee at the bottom of a river. He had been murdered. I had no idea of how or why that happened. I was devastated. It felt strange, too, that this man had given me these texts and now I didn't know what to do with them. So, I started reading them and taking much more interest in what they actually contained.

The mystery of Egypt continued to unfold in me, and Boulder supported my explorations and creative work. Within the year (1980), I began a two-year master's degree in English literature at the University of Colorado at Boulder. In the last year, I enrolled in a translation workshop with professor Sidney Goldfarb, who became a catalyst for writing *Awakening Osiris*. The creative writing teachers at CU Boulder were most helpful in terms of allowing a student to follow her intuition. An excellent translator of Spanish plays, novels, and poetry, Sidney knew the best work came when one had fun with the creative process and with language.

When the time came for students to switch from translating Spanish language texts, he suggested we work in our second language. That seemed easiest for non-native, English-speaking students or for those who already had acquired a second foreign language. But I was neither of these.

"So, what language interests you?" Sidney asked.

Immediately I answered, "Hieroglyphs."

"Why?"

I told him about my friend Robert and the book, and I said that when I was a teenager I hadn't known if I wanted to write or to paint; but hieroglyphic writing seemed to offer both creative possibilities.

"In that case," Sidney said, "get yourself some good grammar dictionaries and some variant translations of the text you want to work on. Compare them, explore them, and like Ezra Pound said, 'Make it new.'" So I did, following Pound's explorations about writing poetry with all of one's senses: image, sound, and narrative.

I began working on the hieroglyphs in the Budge Ani text. On the right-hand side of a journal, I transferred the hieroglyphs of Ani, leaving spaces in between each line. On the left-hand facing page, I copied various translators' works, including Budge, Raymond Faulkner, Miriam Lichtheim, and others. This system left enough room for me to work with what I was seeing, hearing, and researching. Once I had a few of the chapters complete, I showed them to Sidney.

The class ended, but the real work had just begun. Curiosity led me to the university library to study Egyptian religious philosophy, mythology, and history. I explored alternate scripts, metaphysics, and symbolic languages. When time permitted, I allowed myself to simply go to a bookshelf, find a text that intrigued me, then pull it off the shelf and sit down on the floor in the middle of the shelving under a slant of light through the windows to read, to absorb, to digest the mystery of a writer's life. From my spot on the carpet, I'd reach up and pull down other similar books that were next to each other. I spent hours comparing their similar ideas. For weeks that became years, I sat in the narrow aisles between the shelves, reading, taking notes, and deciding which books to check out of the library. Yes, I reshelved the books I wasn't taking in the correct order; I had spent my time in high school as a librarian's assistant and knew the cataloging systems. But at each visit I filled a backpack with more books to study.

The massive inpouring of information and daily meditations stirred my psyche, and I began having incredible dreams. It was as if I'd entered some ancient mystery school. It felt as if most of my work was being done in my sleep. I began dreaming in hieroglyphs. Sometimes, while pouring over the texts laid out on my desk, I'd fall asleep until the moment that my husband opened the screen door outside and let it slam, which shocked me awake. At that moment, the entire meaning of the line of hieroglyphs I had been working on laid itself out in front of me in a flash of images or a scene of great beauty. Sometimes I woke with the scintillating sound of poetry rolling through my head. I thrilled with its symbolism, its puns, its poetry, its myth and magic. How could one language hold such breadth of information?

In just such fashion for nearly eight years, I worked my way through the entire text, beginning to end. Looking for dull, empty spots in the text, I filled them with the earthy, sensual objects of the mythic poetic landscape. The hieroglyphs themselves suggested the images. I worked with the images as symbols, translating the signs into psycho-spiritual keys, as if I were reading tarot. I worked with the construction of the hieroglyphic sentences themselves, finding that the immediacy of the present tense was the basis of hieroglyphic thought. And that thought filled with puns and poetic alliteration and assonance, filled with cadence and repetition of sound and image. There was a musicality to the language, and yet also a great mystery in the pronunciation itself. Few know how to pronounce the Kemetic (ancient Egyptian) language.

Then after that, I returned to the Greek historians and philosophers who so loved Egypt that they (especially Herodotus) tried to retell the mystery narratives of the wisdom keepers of the land. These stories wanted to find a way to return to Egypt and attach themselves to the hieroglyphs from which they had been gleaned like seeds of wheat.

Once I was able to layer all these sounds, images, and myths, I'd return to the text to see what I had left out.

In each reiteration, I found so much more inside this language that I still didn't think I had its translation right. I started from the beginning again, revising and translating it once more—working in the story, the particularity of its nouns, the nuances of image, the ringing sounds of alliteration, repetition, and so on. I translated that book three times. Always it seemed as if there were three different approaches to the same text. Any translator's word-for-word text sounded like gibberish and could never touch the true meaning because English is an abstract language. One word could not grasp the entire play and depth of the hieroglyphs, which eloquently speak in sound and image. They play with the subtleties of symbol, metaphor, and poetry, touching at the edges of myths without really stopping to relate the full story, or even a version of the story. The Egyptians were not linear thinkers. They embedded the stories within the glyphs themselves, using allusions to suss them out.

I fell in love with this mysterious text. I fell in love with its culture—in love to the point that it felt almost like having a mistress. I wanted to spend all my time on it, to sink down into soft hours of night turning into the crystalline light of dawn, writing—all the while, the book emerged from the dark underworld into light. How poignant seemed the Coming Forth by Day. I had to steal away in secret to be with it, timidly getting out of bed so as not to disturb my sleeping partner. My relationship to the text overwhelmed my everyday life.

When I began working with the texts, I was single; then I married, had a baby, and was trying to hold down a job as a tech writer, and later as a book editor, all while still managing to spend enough time with these glyphs. Trying to squeak hours out of a day became exhausting, so I arranged to hypnotize myself to get up at four in the morning and work for two hours before the baby woke up, before I had to get dressed, and before I went to work. Yes, it was obsessive. But the text had me so deeply that I didn't want to do anything else. If my husband or baby woke before the text and I had our time together, I despaired.

It took a long time to complete this work. I loved every moment of feeling its energy sing in glorious exultations all the way down into my bones. Once I finished the translation, beginning to end, I would turn the book over and begin again at the front, retranslating, enriching, drawing up the sensual and essential mystery of the Egyptian world, of nature, of child and rock and sky and light. I filled six copy books with translations that only I and a few magazine editors were reading.

During those years, I lived beneath the Flatirons, which seemed as if they were a majestic memory of a very familiar landscape in which I had, once upon a distant lifetime ago, stowed myself away, a landscape that had yet to reveal itself to me in this lifetime. But an afterimage of a past life must have pressed itself into my brain, for when I stepped off the train in Denver in 1978, I saw for the first time those jutting sun-drenched distant foothills and mountains against the blue cloth of sky, and I knew I had come home again. I had to live there, because this scenery felt so familiar, but I had no idea where or when I had been there, or why. Perhaps that feeling was a past-life memory bleeding through into this lifetime.

How did I know Egypt's specific topography, geography, and spirituality without ever having been there? Egypt was already in my bones.

A time came when my husband said, "This is crazy. I can't live like this. Everyone thinks you are crazy." He argued that I was living in a fantasy and that I really needed to pay attention to my day-to-day life. Rejecting anything that smacked of religion and feeling shut out of my life, he said, "You know, you should just forget all that stuff. Just throw it away. Show me that you care about me."

He had a point. I said, "Yeah, you're right."

One night after we'd had another big row, I finally felt beaten down. "Okay," I agreed. "I'll get rid of them." I packed up all of the books that Robert had given me. I gathered my manuscript, which was tons of paper by this time, all of my notes, *The Book of the Dead*—everything; I put it all in a cardboard box on the back seat of my car. As I was driving uphill through town toward the dumpster, I glanced in my rearview mirror. There in the backseat of my car sat Robert. He didn't look like the Robert I remembered on earth. He looked distinctly priest-like with a bald, shaved head and a white linen robe. But I knew it was Robert.

I thought, "Naaah. This must be the power of suggestion or something. I'm not going to pay any attention to this." So, I kept driving; and just as though Robert knew that I did need to pay attention, he reached out and touched my shoulder. I'd never experienced anything like that in my life. It felt as if I had stuck my hand in an electrical outlet. I just started shaking as quivers of electricity shot up and down my body. I momentarily lost consciousness, but I remember screaming. It didn't sound like a Hitchcock horror movie scream. It sounded like a scream that came from beyond time. It seemed to stretch way out and reverberate: *Wah-aoo-aoo-aooo . . .*

Somehow, I managed to stop the car. I looked in the rearview mirror again, and he was still there. I kept looking and looking at him, waiting for the image to fade, but it didn't. Then I said, "Goddamn it, Robert. Don't you ever do that to me again. You scared the hell out of me!" The minute I said that, he was gone. Poof! He just disappeared. I sat there for a while, until I finally took the spare tire out of the wheel well and put the stuff in the box in it. I covered it with the rug and the spare wheel, then turned around and drove home. Thereafter, I worked on the material during my lunch hour, pulling the copybooks and material out one at time.

By the time I had finished translating the book for a third time, I received a letter from a man I didn't know—a friend of a friend. He said he had seen some of the work in print in a magazine while he was just beginning his new press. He asked me if I had translated the entire book and, if I was nearly finished with it, could he take a look at it.

Sure thing.

That was David Fideler from Phanes Press. The way in which all of this happened seemed entirely magical. The question had never been when did I become interested in Egypt, but when did Egypt become interested in me? Somehow, it crooked a finger at me and beckoned. I followed the mystery for forty years, and it never let me go.

Every major event in my life has been that cosmic finger pointing at me, saying, "You will do this."

More than learning a process for reading and interpreting the glyphs, the fall into the magic of Egypt has taught me just how deeply we need to be shocked to be awakened because, truly, I was asleep. Even though I had this book and the library of information spread out before me, I was still asleep, until that moment when Robert slipped between the worlds and into the backseat of my car.

In June 1989, when I was between jobs and my daughter was nearly four, my then mother-in-law Wanda Stefanidis was living in Athens with her husband, Themos, a port captain. Wanting to see her granddaughter, she bought tickets for the three of us to come to visit her in Greece. She invited us for the entire summer. I immediately also made plans to meet my friend Virginia for a week in Cairo, just a jump across the Mediterranean, leaving my husband and daughter in Athens with his family.

In preparation for the Egypt trip, I travelled to Eleusis, whose oracular mysteries and history were all built around the Egyptian mysteries of Osiris and Isis. As I approached the cave of Persephone, I carried an inscribed and signed copy of my book *Awakening Osiris* wrapped in a plastic Ziploc bag that also contained an offering prayer of gratitude for the gift of this work. I asked Osiris and Isis, as well as Persephone and Hades, to bless the work I had done and was giving back to them for safekeeping. Then with every ounce of strength I had, I pitched the book as far back into the recesses of that cave as I could.

Unfortunately, my friend Virginia had a medical emergency that prevented her from meeting me in Cairo. Thus, I began my first trip through Egypt alone. This solo venture off the Greek mainland was made possible due to publishing *Awakening Osiris*. That first royalty check purchased a week of travel in Egypt. When I stepped off the plane, I felt an urge to kneel and kiss the ground. What a wonder it was to see at last the land that had already become a familiar landscape—learned from photographs and now steeped in dreams and reverie. I reveled at the hoopoes jumping about the tufts of grass growing up between the cracks on sand-covered sidewalks, the children riding white donkeys and sucking on sugar cane pulled from the donkey's load, the date palms spreading their shade over the rows of cabbages. I felt I knew this place.

Riding the train through a mystical night of desert starlight reflected on large swathes of emptiness, I woke suddenly at dawn, as if I'd been yanked out of sleep by an invisible hand. I thrust open the heavy curtains just as the train passed the cliffs of Nag Hammadi, north of Qena and Luxor. The sky seemed an infinite turquoise stone, and the dawn light painted the cliffs a specific sunrise peach. These sunlit cliff faces seemed exact renditions of the Flatirons along the Front Range of Boulder, Colorado, an image upon which I had gazed every dawn for eight years while composing *Awakening Osiris*. Overwhelmed, I broke into tears, as if I had known that place outside Qena and been there a thousand times. I had no idea how dramatically my life would change from this date forward.

The book was picked up by Audio Renaissance, who asked Jean Houston to voice the audio book. I selected certain passages, then a few months later I enrolled in her Estes Park, Colorado, mystery school, hoping to meet her. A friend introduced us at the opening. I was a bit sheepish; but she threw her arms around me in the biggest hug, and then she stood back to look at me. "Oh Lady," she said, "you have no idea who you are." She told me about reading my work in Chicago at a recording studio with her partner Peggy, and how tears literally flowed from their eyes as she read my work. Then she gave me the greatest gift of all—her friendship and support. It felt as if she had lifted up a rock and found me under it—this exotic Kentucky hillbilly with an innate heart wisdom that had been carved upon the rocks of Egypt.

In 1991, Jean invited me to travel to Egypt with her, along with ninety others, which allowed me to prepare and become ready to lead my own tours to the sacred sites in the future. From Cairo to Abu Simbel and even through Middle Egypt, it seemed the texts in the tombs and on the temple walls rattled through me, and the places we travelled awakened deep memories. I am sure that Jean could see that it would.

At various places, she would step off the bus, lean over to me, and whisper, "Tell us, Normandi. Why are we here?" Then the stories came out, the myths, the history, and the remnants of ancient poetry. I cannot thank Jean enough. As much as Robert gave me the hieroglyphs, Jean gave me permission to continue to spend my life completing the translations from the inside out. I spent several years working with her and her husband Robert Masters on various projects, including helping her with her Egyptian book, *The Passion of Isis and Osiris*.

On that trip, I roomed with an older friend, June Sampson, whom I had met at Jean's mystery school. I knew her husband had Alzheimer's, and June had been his life support and touchstone for many years during his illness. She had put off her own wishes and desires, so when the opportunity to travel to Egypt with Jean, Peggy, and me presented itself, she informed her daughters that they were responsible for her husband's care.

We had no sooner checked into our hotel rooms in Cairo when June was told that Edgar had died. Given the choice of returning home or staying in Egypt, she chose Egypt, saying, "I've spent years telling Edgar goodbye." I agreed to help her mark his transition by creating a ritual in every temple in Egypt, an appropriate reading from *Awakening Osiris,* and an instruction about a hieroglyphic symbol, one of the amulets on the wall that would assist the soul in its passage through the underworld and aid its coming forth into light.

Since then, many people touring Egypt have led their groups or themselves through the ritual of Coming Forth into Light by reading from *Awakening Osiris.* They write me to say they have found its poetry uplifting, as I had hoped it would be, and therapeutic to their process, as I felt writing it had been to mine. It has been used in weddings (Jean married a couple in Abydos using the words scripted from my book); in dream temples and hypnagogic states (Patricia Monaghan and I led a group of participants in an Egyptian dream incubation by having designated individuals waking and reading continuously from the book all through the night); and countless people say that they have used it as part of the text funerals and memorials.

I once received a letter from a deejay in Colorado thanking me for the book, which he read to his mother during her transition. He could not leave his job, so he had a family member tune the radio to his station while his mother was in hospice in Wyoming. He played intermittent music and read to her for his entire shift that day and the next until she passed. It moved me very much to hear this story.

Nicki Scully, my dear friend and colleague, once told me that before I knew her, she had received a copy of my book. When her dear friend, Jerry Garcia of the Grateful Dead, died, she said that she approached his casket and read to him, in particular, "Becoming the Phoenix," which she told me was his favorite passage while he was alive.

Nicki and I first met sometime in the mid-1990s, when I began receiving calls from people inviting me to attend events or to travel with them. She cold-called me, asking if I would join her in a performance venue in San Francisco. The dance rehearsals of "The Bath" directed by

Rhea Lehman were among my favorite events—the first of future dance and theatrical performances based on the book; yet that performance was cancelled by the promoter before it ever came to pass. Still, the work brought me into resonance with Nicki's work and she became a multi-decade-long collaborator.

That collaboration found us traveling together through Egypt for nearly two decades. We were drawn together in her shamanic mystery school through *Awakening Osiris*. More than anyone, she gave me a return ticket "home" to Egypt. Every summer for nearly two decades, we created a gorgeous summer Egyptian mystery school in Eugene, Oregon, working through and completing initiations in her temple, vision questing, and performing rituals. The culmination of that work became our collaborative book *The Union of Isis and Thoth*. She and I learned so much through each other.

Let me say clearly that in the process of wanting to become a writer, I was the beneficiary of many gifts from Sprit. I was gifted this book from Egypt herself, and even the death of Robert Weiler became a gift because his life touched mine, and the mystery of how that happened led from one thing to the next. I was gifted a scholarship from the Creative Writing program at the University of Colorado, where I met Sidney Goldfarb, and I was gifted a mystery school scholarship from Jean Houston, then a trip to Greece and Egypt by my mother-in-law. I was gifted publication by magazines and finally by the Phanes Press publisher, David Fideler. All allowed me the opportunity to be uplifted and supported in my quest.

I am not recounting my glory days. I am recounting the surprises and the gifts that befell me and continue to shower down upon me. I recount them with a heart full of deep, deep gratitude. The mystery of this book, its voice that moved through me, has been such a blessing these last forty years in more ways than I can enumerate. This book has been my life. It is a record of my desires and thoughts, just as any spiritual diary or book of the afterlife is built upon the life lessons gleaned from the world. It pleases me that the book remains relevant to others. If you are reading this, you bless me with your attention. As the ancient Egyptians would say, "Say my name that I may live."

> From the power that binds all beings
> That man frees himself who overcomes himself.
>
> —GOETHE GEHEIMNISSE

1

The Return

STARS FADE LIKE MEMORY THE instant before dawn. Low in the east, the sun appears golden as an opening eye. That which can be named must exist. That which is named can be written. That which is written shall be remembered. That which is remembered lives. In the land of Egypt Osiris breathes. The sun rises and mists disperse. As I am, I was, and I shall be a thing of matter and heaven.

On a midsummer's day a rustle of beetles fly singing from dry grass to raise the sun like a dung ball. In the sky bright as Nut's belly above her lover, the sun glints like yellow jasper. The body of heaven lies smooth and firm as an egg. It is joy to lick the wind. On countless mornings I see the fireball roll and tears roll down my cheek. The souls of men like tears from Ra stream down the face of heaven. The eye of the great one sees how stars fade.

Osiris returns from the mountain of sand to the green land of his birth. Morning comes to Egypt. Across an expanse of dirt and stone, cool shadows strain toward the mountain where in dry tombs the dead are yawning, wondering who has lit the temple fire and who has brought sweet cake. I, Osiris, rise and hurry into the two lands of the living. Black earth and red earth join by a buckle of sky. I embrace the double horizon. I embrace the two mountains, the east and west. I am god of the living and dead, embracing my soul and shadow.

The ka of Osiris grows bright wings. His face glows with white heat. Above fields, I speak with the voice of a hawk, my eye sharp as a blade against the wheat. I speak the word from which I was made. I speak of truth and splendor and strength, of the honor of death and power of return. I speak of the crested ibis.

Where gods have gathered, the heart grows still. A procession of jabiru walk, laying the eggs of other lives, of blue souls in another time. Incense rises where gods gather. Heaven and earth are long dreams weighed in the balance. A man is known by his words and deeds. Beautiful is the new sun sailing in a river of sky in the boat of morning. Beautiful is man in his moments in time, a thousand beads of thought on a white string.

Darkness gives way to light, dumbness to speech, confusion to understanding. Devourers of the dead are given their own dry bones to eat. The worm that would suck the eye of Ra has been pierced by spears of light. His green heart has been pitched into the fire; it sizzles like rotten meat.

The old man's house is a riot of living. In bright corners children are singing because their mother has given birth. The world is made new with laughter. The strings of the lyre hum. The sun floods the country and cities with light. Boats sail on emerald waters. Fish have returned to spawn. In the field a stubborn donkey sleeps, though his master thrashes him with a stick. I laugh because I have come home. I am content with the movement of hours.

This is the meaning of yesterday—that friends remember my name and after long journeys I am greeted by their voices on the road. They embrace my hands and feet. Look what corn and grapes we share. Look what abundance of meat. Under the eye of the great one the children of Egypt gather. Her four winds gather—mountain dwellers, basket weavers, potters and musicians.

In my life I've known the love of men and seen gods on their slow barges passing. The ka of Osiris walks where he pleases. I am thought, shadow, bone. I am the black ibis pecking at corn and the blade of a hunting knife. I am the guardian of sun and moon, the falcon that flies between them. I shall be given day and night and all the space therein. In the bark of morning and the bark of evening I shall gain passage to hidden things. Law and truth, memory and time shall be my sails and rudders.

This is the going forth of gods into the land of triumph. The river is emerald and filled with light. The course of this boat is true. Inside my people has always lived the grace of bullrushes growing. Like a fruit tree sprung up by the river Nile, from my names rises the story of Egypt.

That which is written shall be remembered. Osiris lives in the land of his birth.

2

Greeting Ra

THIS DAY I AM WITH YOU. Stabbed by the light of the great mind
I wake. The sun crests the hill and the hawk, according to a higher will,
whirls and circumscribes day. I am called from my house. I shuffle sand
underfoot, but my heart leaps. I open, am pierced by light. A cry escapes
my lips. I know not what I say; it is the language of soul beneath skin, the
song of birds in acacia trees.

Beautiful is the golden seed from which the corn arises; beautiful the sun
on the hill from which springs god's day. My body nourishes some unfolding time and purpose. I shine bronze as Hathor's mirror. My heart lifts like
the sun. Passion and power quiver on the land, casting long shadows.

Now the people in their houses stir, yawning, shouting, stretching.
Shot through with light, they glow and quiver. Stones of sunlight pile up
in heaven. Emerald is truth when god draws near. Blessed are we by sun.

Ra is the child, a golden knot of flesh dropped from open air, bright
star in the dark house of Osiris, heir to the ages, word edged into world. He
grows a long beard and sits on the mountain, knowing its secrets. He rises
from the flood. Drawing up water, he quenches the thirst of his people. They
drink and enter the river. He sucks the breast of heaven, golden-haired, flesh
on fire. Always burning, returning, always constant and new.

It is his breath we breathe, his love that endures, his power that moves
the world. We are the quivering of his arrows, the stirring of his hands.
We are his spirit moving in matter. May the eye of god pierce us and give
us the grace of his will. We are held in god's hands. Like the ocean, we
whirl and remain the same. We are bound by law and held by the truth of
change, that all seasons return, and that which was once and is no more
shall come again.

Sing then, rejoice and bind yourself to god's will. See how the seed falls from the tree and is buried. Die at once and live again. You shall grow like that sycamore, rooted in matter, bound for boundless sky. You shall be blown by wind. You shall see the storm and sing its praises. You shall lie in the fields and kiss the earth. Raise your arms. You shall see the fury and power of god and change forever.

Drink the cup of heaven. Let grace roll down your head like water. Drink in earth; take in the things of the world. The barley grows straight in rows; the young shoots unfurl according to a higher purpose. Truth rides visibly through the world. Have you not seen it? The sun shimmers with the power of gold. We are breathless in golden air. Drink in the light and praise the cup of forever that spills out the threads of eternity.

Ra is an old man walking the world, as much with the earth as the skin of a snake. He is with us, the spirit, the gold, the god, the ebb of life, watcher over the world. We rise like swallows and fly up the ladder of heaven. We sit in his hand. He buries us in the blue egg of the world. We are pressed into the soil and rise. We grow in him. The world changes, and god and men. We spin and sing in the house of sun. The earth is glad. Cows chew the cud of light. We breathe the perfume of a golden flower. Old men and women rise, burst from their houses, arms lifted, dancing, crying, singing. Dawn is a lyre playing the song of day.

Ra rises. He goes out into the world, a passion, a fire burning up night, making day. His light ennobles the face of heaven. He warms the belly of sky. He gladdens Nut, his mother. He walks the upper regions, his heart inflamed with love. The waters in the pool of the farthest oasis are calmed. He gathers the sand serpents to his breast. He fears no living thing. He made them, what is known and not known. He speaks their names and takes their venom. The snake who gobbles the world enters Ra. Burned in fire, he vomits the evil he has spoken. His words are smelted into gold. With a kiss, Ra turns poison into magic. He twines the snake about him. Now death lives on his forehead, side by side, with light. Let breath come and go. Let the great world change. Let men see that serpents entwine the god as the light of god entwines each man. It brushes his lips with sunlight, with kisses of life, kisses of death, kisses of joy, kisses of poison and magic.

The evening boat draws near. Ra comes to meet it at the edge of sky, the edge of river, the thin blade of time. It arrives and he steps from the shore of knowing. He enters. Small waves rock the boat and the stems of reeds are bowing. He sails off: north, south, east or west. He travels lightly toward the other shore of time. Infinity is his. Behold! a star has entered sky. The geese take flight across a waxing moon. Oh substance, understanding of earth, creature of becoming making himself understood. Flames of fire lick his body like golden serpent tongues, like the mouths of women in love. The wind uplifts him. He sings a dark song gliding toward dusk in the boat of evening. We show him our hands, the magic he placed in them. His boat slices water. He passes towering papyrus. Three godlike ducks wade in and follow. They glide, turn and spiral. Three godlike sparrows swoop and spin above the banks. Even the frogs are dancing and singing.

Ra rules the air and the gods invisible. The book of law lies in his hands. The speech of his lips falls lightly into being. His word enters the world. "Creation," says he. "Destruction. Power invisible. Glory. The house of heaven is the house of man. No walls stand between heaven and earth. You are no farther from me than from your own hot breath." At any moment you enter heaven by saying, "I am a temple of Ra." Love is his light; compassion the light of the world. Ra is fire. Joy is the sky. His heart beats with forever. The white clouds of his thought pass over the sky and water.

3

Greeting Osiris

THAT QUIVERING EVENING STAR IS HIS; blue eye of the watcher; body of Osiris, heart, mind and soul of a god awake in the darkening world. Here, where the sun and sorrow stop, a man may sit long by the river, let water flow through his fingers like history, the ageless Osiris, watch corn rise up and dream vegetal dreams. Or, he may hold grains of sand in the palm of his hand, count and name them "everlasting." The god is walking, walking, a million years; the beat of his left foot, his right—the flux of the universe. He hurries on, going somewhere, running messages between gods and men, propelled by the power in his feet.

Blessed be Osiris. Blessed be the son of earth sprung from the egg of the world, the great cackler. Blessed be the son of heaven, dropped from the belly of sky. Blessed is his birth, five days of peace won from the hands of gods. He is light, the white crown, the ain soph, the joy of becoming in heaven and earth, the father of men and angels. He takes the gold crook and makes himself shepherd. He takes the silver flail and makes himself judge. The power of his divine fathers encircles his spine, as the snakes entwine the caduceus. His heart is hidden fire; it burns a hole in the mountain. He guides his people to the light.

"Come," he says. "I come in the power of Light. I come in the light of Wisdom. I come in the mercy of the Light. The Light has healing in its wings."

He is Nebertcher, the infinite, lord of the universe. The words of becoming taste sweet to his tongue. That which was ravaged is made whole in him; seeds are planted and the earth greens. He is Tahersetanef who walks backwards into yesterday, a man of secrets in a world hidden away. His footsteps are possibility. That which is follows in stride and that which is not yet flows behind him as his shadow. He is Seker, never seen nor looked upon, the benevolent face of darkness, the good death that men call upon, the end, the beginning of truth. He is Osiris, the dark and terrible eye, the broken body and scattered limbs, the smell of rotten flesh, the knowingness and finality of death. He judges the souls of men. He is Unnefer, and he endures forever upon a road bordered by flowers. He sits long by the waters, hears its music, becomes its song. He smiles, time passing, lost in dream.

Blessed be the god in his names, salvation of priests and goatherds, king of kings, lord of lords. He counts the hairs on every man's chin. Celestial fire descended, he steps down lightly onto earth. He hears the prayers of all men, animals, angels. He hears the dead murmur with their mouths full of sand. He uplifts the sky, rents the veil, reveals the temple. His flesh is burnished bright as copper. The eyes in his head are like blue stones underwater, lapis lazuli. Priest and man, his body shimmers turquoise green.

He is solitude and perfection, ether and atmosphere at all times and in all places. His body widens and his people are welcomed into it; his embrace is sleep. He is fire dancing about the heads of dreamers, the instant of forever that sparks poets and lovers. He turns his beautiful face in the dark. He flows quietly away on subterranean waters.

His is the splendor of heaven, strength of earth, triumph over the worm. His is the mind of ibis, the intelligence, in his bones the instinct of animals, in his blood the pulse of iron. He is the elemental made eternal, the upright pillars of temples, the trunk of sycamore trees. The living soul of land, he is matter and mind taking form. He is what he imagines, divine, a spark thrown into dust. The winds swirl above a city of sand. Eternal in essence, he transmutes. He is death, a phoenix, a fire raging, changing, going in and coming out of form in time. He is a mad genius wind howling and the beat of winds, individual and inspired. He is one god or else he is two old men walking, leaning on their sticks, conspiring. He is hell become heaven, becoming hell; he is evolution, a matter of energy, a star in the dark tomb, a shadow cast by sunlight. He is life that cannot be contained, a holy insurrection, blessed negativity.

I am with him. I am like that old Osiris waking in the night. Drunk on the cool wine of darkness, I eat the bread of life and die. I know. I am blessed by mortality. I am a field enduring, growing wheat one year, barley the next, tangled flowering papyrus, a hill of sand. I am everafter, changing, while the eye of the watcher shines and takes me in.

4

The Speeches

I CROSS AN OPEN FIELD of stones shaped all like hearts and say to the rocks: this one shall break, and this hold the rain, and this one be still, and this other crumble and its grains of sand shall mark my passage. Beat. Beat. Beat. The power of my Self is moving. My heart. My birth. My coming into existence. My passions. My indifference. The sun within warms me; the heart enlightens the intellect. I am my Self coming forth, a creature bearing light.

May I stand amazed in the presence of god. May the rhythm of my heart stir music that enslaves darkness. May my heart witness what my hands create, the words I utter, the worlds I think. May my flesh be a sail propelled by the breath of dream. May I ride in calm waters toward destiny. May life flow through me as the seed from the phallus flows, with a shout of joy, life begetting life.

May I stand in the midst of celestial fire until my heart is molten gold. May twelve goddesses dance every day about me, a circle of flesh aflame. May I spin among them, my face flushed with heat. May I walk on earth radiant, everywhere complete. May the omniscient eye observe my deeds and know the law my heart knows, the zodiac of men and beasts alive, the call of angels, the word. May my body bend toward the will of the heart. May I not think and act diversely. May truth rest on me light as a tail feather dropped from a falcon in cloudless sky.

Thou spirit within, you are my Self, my power, my ka, the fire of god. May I create words of beauty, houses of wonder. May the labor of my hands be mirrors unto god. May I dance in the gyre and draw down heaven's blessing. May I be given a god's duty, a burden that matters. May I make of my days a thing wholly. May I know myself in every pore of skin. May the god's fire burn in my belly and heart. May I be stronger than these bones and bits of flesh. May my health be the wholeness of divinity.

On earth I walk daily before the gods, but in the house of heaven my feet are still. There is no need for haste. My heart is a lyre that hums. My lungs fill with the breath of fire. A cool breeze encircles me. I rest in god's bosom here, while on earth my hands are busy. And when work is done, I return to the heart afire, center of the universe, peace, unto god.

I remember the names of my ancestors. I speak the names of those I love. I speak their names and they live again. May I be so well-loved and remembered. In truth, may the gods hear my name. May I do work with my hands worth remembering.

I am an old man travelling amid strange cities and faces. I've prayed in temples from the plains to the delta. In Hermopolis, beneath the crumbling feet of a statue, I found this heart of stone, encircled in bronze, ringed all in silver, made of lapis lazuli. It was inscribed in iron by the god in the god's own hand before the dawn of history, and it was this book wherein lay the law that is. It was the secret name of god. And I lay the stone heart upon my own that I might memorize it, that its words might be etched into my being. Great is the nothingness, the all that is. I am a being of light.

Thoth speaks:

> *The ibis and the ink pot—these are blessed. For as the ibis pecks along the bank for a bit of food, so the scribe searches among his thoughts for some truth to tell. All the work is his to speak, its secrets writ down in his heart from the beginning of time, the gods' words rising upward through his dark belly, seeking light at the edge of his throat. We are made of god stuff, the explosion of stars, particles of light, molded in the presence of gods. The gods are with us. Their secrets writ only in the scrolls of men's hearts, the law of creation, death and change inscribed in the blood and seed of man's love. In the beginning and at the end, the book is opened and we see what in life we are asked to remember.*

Hear, then, my words, the ringing of my speech, as the heart and the scroll of this life fall open. Truth is the harvest scythe. What is sown— love or anger or bitterness—that shall be your bread. The corn is no better than its seed, then let what you plant be good. Let your touch on earth be light so that when earth covers you, the clods of dirt fall lightly. The soul of a man forgets nothing. It stands amazed at its own being. The heart beats the rhythm of its life. The lungs breathe the ions of its own vibration. The mind recalls its thoughts. The glands respond to its emotions. The body is a soul's record. And when a man's life ends, his body is given back to gods and the gods shall see what use their laws have been. They shall see the deeds its hands have made, the sparks of light its heart set in the world. They shall see whether or not their love, their powers have been wasted, whether the plants it has grown were nourishing or poison. And like the ibis, the gods shall circle about him, hunting for seeds that remain uncultivated, for ideas that lie dormant, thoughts left unexpressed. They shall find new seeds from the plants he has tended. And these shall be planted again in the clay of a new man and he shall be sent back to the world until all the gods have seen fit to create in man is cultivated, and then, in final death, he shall be welcomed home as one of them.

The gods speak:

Let the great wheel turn. We sit at the hub of the universe and the stars spin around. A man's fortunes rise and decline. He makes plans and his plans are changed. When the moon is full, it shall grow thin. Some days it's easier to commune with gods than others. Bless the wheel where all things spin. This is the story of a life. A man learns nature is not always kind. Nature acts according to nature. Crocodiles eat fish and no one can be blamed. A man takes his fortunes in stride. Swaying first to his left foot and then the right, he learns to walk and hold his balance. He sees that gods surround him, but most days he walks his path alone. With one foot always forward, a man reaches heaven.

The oar is in the water and the boat glides along. The seeds are planted, the ideas, the inspiration; the words rise like wheat from his mouth. Let one's speech be thoughtful so that small things said unthinkingly shall not fall as bad seed and sprout vines that surround him. A man reaps what he sows. What he dreams of shall come to pass. Before the world formed it was the Great One's idea, and so a man is careful about what he wishes. He knows his death is but another harvest. His life is spent nourishing his people. He saves seeds for the future. He offers up life and gives the gods their due. We've not seen the last of him. He is not greedy and so has all he needs—all the love, the joy, the days. When he hungers, there is bread. When he thirsts, the water is cool. He gives himself and the Self is given to him. He comes and goes in the presence of gods. He is given a field to tend and he tends it, therefore, his harvest is plentiful. As he cares for his children, so is he cared for in his old age. What goes around comes around, and so the great wheel turns.

Horus speaks:

I am life rushing on, born from the egg of the world, from the belly of a magic woman, born of my father's dreams. I am the screech of wind, the rush of falcon wings, talons sharp as knives. I came after you. I stand before you. I am with you always. I am the power that dispels darkness. Look upon the dark face of my father, Osiris. He is nothing. Embrace him. Even nothing cannot last. The seed laid into the void must grow. The candle's only purpose is to shine in the darkness. Bread is meant to be ground to pulp in the teeth. The function of life is to have something to offer death. Ah, but the spirit lies always between, coming and going in and out of heaven, filling and leaving the houses of earth. A man forgets, but his heart remembers—the love and the terror, the weeping, the beating of wings.

I am an Osiris, a man waking in the night, listening to the varied voices of stars. The gods speak through me and I am one of them. Yet, at times, they seem to shine so far away from me. Some days I push the plow, gather corn, make bread for the children, dig wells and wait for them to fill; and nothing of my life seems holy. It is only labor, sweat drying on sun-burnt skin. I go on believing in miracles. I bend my back and lift heavy stones, legs trembling, and I strive to believe it when I say, "I do the work of gods. The fields will be cleared. The temples will be built." If I were an animal perhaps I could be happy, untortured by bitterness, unconfused by what I think. I am learning to master thought, to do as I say I do, to say I feel what I feel. I am not angry when I speak gentle words. I do not beat the donkey and call myself beloved of gods. Truly, I strive to carry the load without noticing the burden, to be on this hot earth a cool jug of water, to stand in the wind like sturdy sycamore branches, a place where birds rest, where cattle gather, where sap rises, wherein earth and sky are home.

5

Coming Forth by Day

THE FOREPAW OF A LION, the forearm of a man, the primal ray of sun. I wake in the dark to the stirring of birds, a murmur in the trees, a flutter of wings. It is the morning of my birth, the first of many. The past lies knotted in its sheets asleep. Winds blow, flags above the temple ripple. Out of darkness the earth spins toward light. I feel a change coming. My thoughts flicker, glow a moment and catch fire. I come forth by day singing.

Blessed are the cattle asleep in the fields. They shake their horns, tearing the dream. Blessed are the bulls waking, their first thoughts of creation. This day I make myself anew. I create life; my flesh coils about me foot to head. My breath rushes through and my blood. The mind sparkles, dances, the world whirls beneath the sun. I am given to know things I knew not yesterday. I burn like a god aflame, sail my boat upstream at dawn, pushing on quietly among the reeds, softly.

For you I light a fire in the sky. My love dispels darkness. I place the pot over the fire, add water, flour and meat. We shall nourish each other with words and bread. Born of stars, of pale moonlight skimming mountaintops, we are men and women exchanging glances at the crossroads. I am born of sky, filled with light. I darken. I am various as weather. I am predictable as sunrise, moonset, the winds that blow, breathtaking as Sirius rising. I am for you. I am the utterer of your name. Speak of me often and we shall live.

I am a thought that came to pass. Long believed, I live forever. I am words repeated often. I am a happy man. I am a blessed man. I am a perfecting man. I am love and shall endure forever. I am a thankful man, a man of peace, poetry, dream. I am a well-fed man. I am a dancing man beloved of gods. I am an old man who has lived long. I am heading home.

I am an old tree by the Nile banks. A thousand birds nested in my branches and beneath, women cooled themselves from the sun. Years passed. I grew slowly and with grace. This earth I love, the water, the sky. Tomorrow I fall and, at last, the women with baskets on their heads shall make a passage across the river. They will speak for the first time in years to the women on the opposite bank. They will clasp hands and hold their voices to whispers. They shall marvel at each other's faces. And that will be as good a death as any for me, with women weeping, lotus blooming, and cool breezes blowing. That will be a victory. And so on, through the ages, have I been useful and loved.

I come forth by day. I go out burning. To the end, I burn white with heat. On the day of unwrapping the mummy cloths, on the day of opening the storehouse, on the day of washing the body, on the day of speaking secrets, I am with you, my love, as gods are. I stand beside you at the lotus pool watching that pink bud ready to flower. It is I, Osiris. I am joyful as a stone. It is not the joy of men I feel; it is the joy of matter. I am a presence. I am of the world. I am magic. I went the circuitous path of the unseen, from nothing but thought into becoming. I am anointed in oil. The power shivers from my heart down into my arms. Self-sacrifice is only learning to make one's self holy, to be the sum of a man, more than his parts. These breaths I release to the wind, make me one with the wind. This blood flows back to the river like water. This flesh dries, it cracks and scatters, dust again. When the light in my eyes flickers out, the spark flies back to the flaming heart of gods. It is only flesh and breath, blood, bones and hair. I come and go out of the fire unchanged.

I am air and flame, water and dust. I am a wick burning in a blue bowl of oil, a fiery sun rising in a tranquil sky. I am the phoenix. I am light. I come forth by day. I am heat burning up mist. I am power, an ancient river overflowing. I am love and memory and sorrow that drift away.

My time is a reflection on the surface of water. A leaf falls and the dream shatters, breaks to pieces; the leaf drifts off. Slowly the waters calm and draw themselves together. And the leaf's life, like a thought, passes from me on the ripple of its own vibration. It enters the world. I am a holy man, not because I am so wise, but because I am a temple of god. I am a priest of the heart. I know what is mine to feel. I let the rain from heaven fill me. I give love away as easily as water.

I am changeable, yes. It is like this. A hummingbird's wings beat so fast he seems to fly standing still. Atoms in the rock whirl about, yet the rock holds together. Lions roar in the temple and the earth trembles. It is only yesterday and tomorrow keeping watch over today. The solid earth like a baby is lifted up to be kissed, to be blessed and set down again. I see things other men don't see. Secret words repeated in mirrors, bits of legend fallen from the lips of slave girls. I gather the greater seed as they thresh their wheat. I am an old priest dancing the mad dance, whirling, whirling, whirling.

I have studied the manifestations of gods and men, and I've seen the dead conversing in thin, reedy voices amid the air. I have read books of magic and made offerings of moly. I have longed to be free, to rise up as smoke from earth into air. I am a priest of change.

I am a priest of love, a courtier enchanted by the slender ankles of women, by bells and incense, dances and gauze. Beneath the moon my boat rocks gently. I scoop up fish by the fistful and feed the ibis outside the temple. I remember to weave my garlands of onions and flowers on feast days. I plant my seeds and carry god in my hands through the fields to bless them. I drag the large stones to higher ground and write prayers to last forever, songs to gods and creations, women and kings. I have turned the spade and smelled the black moist secret smell of earth and I knead the clods gently in my hand. They are supple and innocent as woman. In the right season, I plant my seeds.

Oh spirits that guide a man through the dark halls at death, guide me safely in life past sorrow and depression, steer me from fear and anger and hopelessness. Let me always know the reason for my becoming. Let me hear what gods hear, see what gods see. When the sun is blotted from the sky, let even a small light shine to steer a man's feet. Let me stand in light, bathe in light, clothe myself in light. Let me sit in the lap of gods and hear words of comfort. Oh offerers of cake and bearers of beer, let me not also starve for love, thirst for wisdom. Let my spirit be stronger today than it was yesterday, my heart more peaceful, my mind more fertile, my hands more gentle. Let gods touch my face. Let me go forth shining. Let my feet know the way. Let me walk and pass through fire. Let wild beasts and thieves by the roadside go on sleeping pleasant dreams. Let me pass undeterred into heaven.

For I have made a reckoning of myself, of the things I have done and said and of my intentions; and I long for nothing but to live as a light within, to enter god's heart singing a song so stirring that even slaves at the mill and asses in the field might raise their heads and answer.

6

The History of Creation

IN THE LAND BENEATH I come and go and the earth bends over, wraps its legs around darkness. In black waters boats glide ferrying dead men, gods. It is quiet here, full of stars and boats that slice the water, slick river dripping from every oar. Men whisper, women . . . or are they only my selves? Is the world at ease? Do I dream it? I've come somehow through this veil of mist. This skin I wear is imagination. I take the shapes of light.

In the great hall, stone lotus pillars rise, light slants in through clerestory windows and incense curls through my beard. I sit alone playing senet, contemplating my path, slow to move one token across the board. I go forth by chance and design, uplifted by faith, beaten down by worry until I make an end to my passage.

I am a hawk with the heart and soul of a man. I fly through the smoke of incensers. I graze the bald heads of priests with lustral wings. I spin above a maelstrom of dancers. I fly up through sunlight. I've the handsome face of a man with black hair, a dark beard. I am a teller of tales, a divinity, a power, a presence.

At first a voice cried against the darkness, and the voice grew loud enough to stir black waters. It was Atum rising up—his head the thousand-petaled lotus. He uttered the word and one petal drifted from him, taking form on the water. He was the will to live. Out of nothing he created himself, the light. The hand that parted the waters, uplifted the sun and stirred the air. He was the first, the beginning, then all else followed, like petals drifting into the pool.

And I can tell you that story.

It was in a world out of time, for there was neither sun nor moon and nothing to mark the night from day until Atum reached down into the abyss and uplifted Ra. The sun shone on Atum's bright face, day began and Ra lived with him from the beginning of time. That was the first day of the world. In gratitude, the sun raised itself and marked the days' flow.

But on that first day, when Atum held the sun, a spark flew out from him. The globe he held caught and reflected first light. The light flew back and he saw the light was himself, he saw that he was god and only after Atum created Ra was he visible even to himself.

In the beginning the earth languished with the sky, nothing lay between them, neither height nor depth, and they were not separate. Each encompassed the other like a lover, and the power of life pulsed between. At a word, Atum parted them and they became heaven and earth so that the sun might move between, that it might ride over and under the bodies of two worlds giving both its light. There was space above and below and between and on all four sides so that all of the things Atum thought might take shape—beast and stone and season.

Yet because they had lain so long together, heaven and earth were still part of each other. Spirit manifested in matter and matter was infused with spirit. Between them ran three pillars of air, earth and water, and these were named thought, form and desire. The spark of his fire pulsed in all of them and this Atum called life. He created himself and his body burned, writhing with dark shapes. Out of himself he created everything else—in a word: the skies, the oceans, the mountains, the plants, the gods and men, and he named them. Of his fire, made of fire, each held fire of its own; therefore, they created and perpetuated life, a cycle of being without end. Man he gave the power to create himself, to name himself and his destiny and to be in it, living eternally in the company of gods. And Atum is with him.

Of fire returning to fire, he cannot be turned away, unless a man extinguishes his light himself, unless he casts out god. If he casts out god, he shall die. He shall be nothing, will be nothing, and will have been nothing. He shall have never existed.

But there is more to this story than the world's creation. There is its destruction.

From fire, out of fire and into fire, Atum takes back what is given. One day he'll destroy what he has created—from nothing returning to nothing. Time shall swallow itself, the lesser days and the eons. How can one remember what never existed?

But today, on this river bank the palm fronds are stirring, Atum lives in light, Ra rises up. There is time for wisdom, deed and possibility. There is yesterday, today and tomorrow. Though we pass quickly, the earth and heaven remain. Let us make something useful with our hands. Though time forgets us, let it not forget our passing. Grant that today we may do work that matters.

I know the future for us all and it is death. As we live we fight sluggishness. We gather our seeds. We put our hearts into the labor of our hands. We make children to live and remember us. We spend our lives preparing for death, for the moment when we offer up our days and labor, our sayings and doings, the sum of ourselves, and beg the gods to call it good.

Like the sun at day's end, we pass west through the gap in the mountains. We go quickly or slowly toward Amentet, the stony plateau. It is only the darkness before light, the hidden place, the house of transformation. It is the slaughterhouse where matter is sliced from spirit, the place where gods are made, the place of fire, of bones, sinew, blood and meat. It is death, the struggle. It is nothing. It is Amentet that makes Ra stand and fight, the last blast of fire we call sunset. It is darkness that makes a man shine brightest. It is the destiny of things in the land of Osiris.

Do you know magic? Can you utter the name of your soul and bring yourself back to light? Can you speak your destiny, create life for yourself from yourself as Atum created Ra? From the light of your works do you know who you are?

I am a phoenix, a soul sparking, a tongue of fire burning up flesh. I consume myself and rise. I am light of the Light, keeper of the book of my becomings: what was, what is, what will be. I am Osiris, a god and the ashes of man. I am the skin he takes on and sheds. I am the cord that binds him from this world to the next. I am his excrement. I am his forms. I am Osiris forever, forever changing, eternal as day, everlasting as night. Can it be said more plainly? Life and death are one. Osiris and Ra.

I am the lightning bolt, the erection, the resurrection and the power of regeneration. I am Amsu, a hare nibbling lettuce. I am a man in love. I am Min, the enumeration of one in the nature of things. I am a child, the rememberer of my father. I am what lives on after the man.

Do you know the story of your birth, how it is like the story of Horus, how Isis wept over the corpse of her husband and her tears were magic and stirred the god's member to rise? They mated and the child was conceived. He was life born out of death, carrier of his father's wisdom. He was the living emblem of love. He was light triumphing over darkness, the first man, the miracle of nature. His was the power of a man to live again not only in deed, but also in the world. He was the healing of the wound. He travelled forth in the world telling the story of his birth, the glory of his father, the goodness of his death. And he was followed by magic. A pair of hawks circled above him. They were his mother Isis and her sister Nephthys. They dropped two plumes which he placed on his forehead, two gifts that fell from the sky—intuition and love, gifts from the goddesses—that he might walk toward heaven and his father and never lose his way.

We are like Horus. We are children of Osiris. We are light defying darkness. He was twice-born—once of sky, once of his mother; that is, once of spirit and once of matter. Having fought cunning and deceit, he came at last to the house of Osiris and was uplifted to heaven. The sun and moon became his eyes. He was light giving light, reflecting light.

That is one story.

Rise up, Osiris. You are an inundation, you are living water, the oar that guides the boat, the delta created by flood. You are the parts of yourself come together. Your child Horus has made an end to your exile. Rise up like corn and nourish the people in a land made fruitful by the word of Atum.

I am an Osiris, too, an old man ready for judgment. I left the city and crossed the plains. Entering the dark house, I cast off doubt and feebleness, I burned up fear, I lit candles and incense. I stand bold before gods, lusting neither for blood nor life nor flesh. I quit the petty concerns of day. It is the hour of my birth, my transformation, my coming into becoming. I anoint myself and rise from the lotus pool. I am changed—a new man, a lapwing among stars. My name is prayer. My spirit hawk flees the egg, leaves its shell. I am fresh as a fledgling in its mother's nest. This life is my offering, what common men give gods.

I am like Ra, born of two worlds in endless space and time. I ride between water and air. I am a word escaped between two lips, desire and thought crystallized into form. I rise from two pools of natron and niter. I rise from the Neterworld. I am the purpose of god, infinite one, multiplicity of his forms. I rise from a green sea of Being; being infinite, I live a million years. I am the action of god's action. I am many things lasting forever. Like Ra himself, I am a child of Atum.

I walked the road toward truth, toward the island between two worlds. I know its beginnings, how it was made, how the land built itself up one grain of sand at a time, how a man's deeds become his fate. And I've seen truth piled up like the thin, worn-out husks of men, skins cast off at the door of the tomb. These burn up and their ashes become god's truth. Blown by wind, the ashes fall and are carried in the stream of unknowing. They form a silt in the river that grows the food that feeds men. So a man's life ended nourishes another; and, depending on his deeds, the food dead men proffer may be poison or nectar.

Some things Atum spoke remain always true: life and death, boundlessness and restraint, intuition and magic, nature and nurture, the earth and sky. His children last forever. The sun rolls ever onward. The doors of heaven open. They open. Light returns to light. The great knowing descends—genius and genesis. His lips part, breath blows over his teeth; the air moves over stones. He tells the story of being and it comes to be. This was the world in the beginning. The fire of god danced on two legs. A beetle rolled its ball over the dark sky. What Atum spoke is holy.

"When I became," said he, "the becoming became. I have become the becoming. I am one seeing myself, divided. I am two and four and eight. I am the universe in diversity. I am my transformations. This is my coming together. Here are my selves become one."

Corn and clouds and cattle are gods renewing. I am the god of myself. Lift me up. Imagination is creation, genius is genesis. The gods give us their hands. Imagination is the fact at the back of the head. I make my changes in secret like an insect in its chrysalis, like lead into gold, the man in his mummy, the sanity in madness. Transformation is intellect, will, purpose, desire. Die. Be born. Bring forth labors and love. Let the invisible be in the visible. Name yourself in your heart and know who you are.

A beetle wanders in the night tasting dust, smelling worms, feeling the ground. He pushes and pushes the seed of himself, a dried ball of dung. Insanity! What can be the fruit of such preoccupation, such slavish devotion to shit? Seeing nothing, hearing nothing, he knows not what he is. He moves not by thought, but by instinct. Through the belly of darkness, he creeps, struggles with his burden, at first small and soft, now a large, hard, heavy stone.

It is one hour before dawn. In the beginning, the end is foretold, but we are not privy to it. We struggle on, strive to reach some end, the purpose of which escapes us, yet, whose purpose is simply that we strive for the end. It is desire that propels us. Process alone has significance. You are one when the question is its own answer, when the answer is the quest. Breezes blow. The ball of dung turns gold. In the light of day, the ball breaks; beetles fly into the sun.

That is Khepera. That is one way of becoming.

There is no creation without destruction. To make the pot to carry water, the river must give up its clay. To make the child, the father must give up his seed. To make love, one gives up the self. Creation is death. Sex is death. All the ways of making are sacrifice. So bit by bit those who create murder themselves, use themselves up, give labor their love.

I know the story of Ra, how in a frenzy of lust for flesh or blood, he cut off his cock with a knife. I know the story of perpetuity, how the death of one is the joy of many. I know the story of holy self-undoing. Salvation. Sacrifice.

There are two passages unto heaven. A seed is planted with the intention of harvest. Its truth is to know the touch of the sickle, to come at last to feed the hand of its reaper. This is the vegetal way of becoming, the law of nature, the way of change, blind function. As barley grows, its leaves open to heaven and its roots burrow deep in the ground. It clings to earth, it clings to life, its end forgotten, denied. The plant must be torn from the ground.

Knowing his end, a man may sacrifice himself, choosing death, rather than life. He feels tomorrow's sorrow, but today's joy; he looks toward heaven and lives without regret. His change quickens, he knows the sorrow of the knife, the ways of darkness. He weeps and clings to the stone near at hand. He lets go. He grieves; therefore, he is man. He becomes the heart and tongue of god. He creates of mortality something immortal. Pain and defeat follow his days, as do joy and passage.

7

The Duel

IN THE LAND BENEATH I come and go and the earth bends over, wraps its legs around darkness. I know the story of creations and the histories of destructions. There were two sons born of heaven and earth and they married beautiful sisters. The world was new then; the fruits of the land were plentiful, the papyrus grew tall and antelope galloped the plains. Through the land a graceful river flowed nourishing all that lay there in it.

The gods said, "I give to you, Osiris and Isis, the land on the northern river; and to you, Set and Nephthys, this land that lies to the south. Go, live in peace and birth sons and daughters. Let them know they are beloved of gods."

In their land Osiris took up the plow and Isis learned to weave. From the labor of their hands came wondrous things—corn, onion and squash, reed baskets and fine linen. But Set in his land stalked antelope and lion. He chased the elephant. He drank animal blood and sucked the marrow of their bones. He tore lettuce from its roots and left nothing to seed, until one day he found his region barren. That day he coveted the bountiful world of his brother. That day sorrow began.

With perfumed hair, amid the jangle of bells on his feet, he came bearing a chest of gold inlaid with emerald, lapis lazuli and green tourmaline. "Lie in the chest, Osiris," he said. "If it fits you, it shall be yours." Distrusting no one, Osiris lay in it. How quickly worked the mind of deceit. Set sealed the chest with his brother in it and carried it to the river. The swift current bore the god away, day grew dark and the night was without stars.

Years passed. Isis found the chest lodged at the core of a tamarisk where the trunk lay thick around it. In a boat she bore the god away, up the Nile far from the marshes to the caves of mountains. There she hid herself, broke open the chest and fell down upon him, chanting spells of love and sorrow. Beneath the long ropes of her hair she worked the magic that conceived the child.

That night Set roamed the mountains hunting jackals by the light of the moon. Stumbling upon the body of his brother in the darkened cave, he shrieked and, enraged, seized the corpse and hacked it into fourteen pieces. Thirteen bits of flesh, bone and sinew—the backbones, the skull, the limbs—he scattered across the Nile, but the tastiest morsel he fed to the crocodile. Lost was the phallus of the god and he would be no more a husband on earth. Hidden and full of form, Isis bore their child in the papyrus swamps. She named him Horus and drew charms of power on his forehead. He grew to converse with his father in dream. He was a mighty son, a golden child, the avenger of his father.

One day the child became a man and that was the day of terror. The battle between gods was waged once in heaven and again and again on earth. When Horus set himself against his uncle, thunder rolled and arrows flashed fire. Beneath the sun's wasting heat, rain fell and dried before reaching the ground. Then the earth rose up like an animal and shook itself. Hot winds blew and stirred the sand into black and red clouds. The sun was blotted from the sky. The two gods seized each other. Blind with rage and stumbling, they fought with magic, with words, with clubs and knives. They fell upon each other with their hands. They wrestled about the earth in the shapes of bears, in the shapes of snakes, in the forms of men and wolves and wild beasts. Swords of iron battered shields of gold. Set buggered the warrior and Horus cut off his balls. They threw vomit and shit in each other's faces.

In heaven the gods wept and looked away, all but Thoth who watched the bloody onslaught for he was unafraid of truth. They might have killed each other, but for the flashing hand of truth which sometimes parted them. They rested. They rose and fought. Years passed. Oh, hideous face of the beast! Looking into his uncle's eyes, Horus saw only himself. The knives thrust into Set came away with Horus' blood. The eye he tore out was the eye of god.

There was a great weeping in the sky. The hair of Ra hung over his face and the world grew blind in the storm. For Ra saw that it was his own flesh, the words he had spoken turned into fists and swords. It was the creation of his own eye that raged against him. The sun fell from the sky and the empty socket dripped blood. Red tears fell scalding the wheat and withering flowers. The sun no longer rose and set. There was no light from it, but neither was there darkness. As the battle waged on even the warrior gods lost strength and they were no more than two angry mists entwined.

Thus, the world was nearly lost until Thoth parted the hair of the sorrowing god and with the fire of his hand brought forth a new eye. It was the living disk of sun—healthy and sound and without defect to its lord, as it was on the first day of the world. It opened and shut and the great wheel turned. The eons to come Thoth inscribed in Ra's blue iris. There he wrote men's fates and of the battles of the gods of dark and light, of Self conquering self.

The heavens are full of eyes—the eye of Horus, the eye of Ra, the eyes of water and of flame. There is the white eye and the black. These are the beautiful eyes of Hathor. These are the eyes of Ptah. Man battles the beast. Order battles chaos. Life strives to conquer death as the eyes of gods and goddesses watch. There are days when a man's own strength is used against him. Even the path of lies can be walked with great persistence. Years passed. Thoth still stands at the river's edge and the battle rages on.

Have you seen it? How the fist of order tries to hold back chaos? How chaos oozes between the grasp of fingers? How the sun is born and dies twelve hours later? How it rises? How the two weights swing in the scale balanced on the fingertip of a god? Envisioned by Ra, Horus and

Set were two possibilities, two sparks of a single eye. The world is whole, the eye of Ra is one crystal and the light of the eye within splinters in a thousand directions. In the underworld Osiris gathers together the fragments of himself.

I am like those warriors Horus and Set when my heart opposes my mind. I am like Osiris, my desires fragmented. I am the pieces of myself, a man longing for unity. I am the guardian of my creations, like Ra whose twin children were Shu and Tefnut, the hot dry air and the mist hanging over the river. The heat of the son's mouth burned up mist, and the hand of the daughter cooled the heat of the air. The doubles walked earth together, each necessary for the other, and the creatures below bade the twin gods homage.

My soul is like the soul of Ra, two spirits in a single heart. Blood rushing in and blood rushing out, the animal is sustained. Mine is the double soul of heaven, the dazzling, splintering power of Ra, the gathering power of Osiris. Mine is the double soul of the universe, heaven mingled with earth. I am a creature of light striving for light, battling ignorance, oppression and darkness. I am matter, the backbone of god. I am the cat beneath the laurel tree, dividing and conquering evil.

There was a day when darkness gathered itself into a hungry snake and crawled upon earth. On her belly she crept toward the city of light, swallowing whatever lay in her path: men and women, beasts, vegetables and gods. And no thing that touched her lips escaped her, for all matter was lost in the darkness. That was the day, or rather the night, that Ra left the sky and took his shape in the cat. To fool the snake, he slept under the leathery leaves of the laurel, holding in his strength, stirring only once for a single languid lick of his paws to brush against his whiskers.

Seeing the cat—that tasty bit of flesh—the snake slithered over and opened its mouth. On the other side of her teeth swelled the void, the abyss, the great nothing, and from it issued the cries of all the lost things of creation. Their voices were a wailing wind that beckoned from the darkness.

Then the soul of Ra in the form of a tiny cat leapt up beneath the shade of the laurel and, with teeth of iron and gold, he snapped off the head of the snake and sliced its body into a thousand pieces and swallowed them up. Blood from the snake's mouth spilled onto the ground. In that manner Ra's creations returned to earth. The blood seeped into the ground and was taken up by the thirsty laurel, which burst into bloom with the souls of the dead in the shape of yellow flowers.

Now leaning down from the east edge of heaven, the god of words had witnessed the battle. He had felt each puncture of the snake's teeth upon his own throat and praised the cat which had given its shape to Ra. "How like the god that made him is the radiant cat. How he slew the darkness with his mouth!" And Mau became the cat's name and the god gave him words of power.

I have stood on the eastern bank beneath that flowering laurel—it is old now; its roots gnarled but still bursting with life—and I have gazed at the sky seeing daily the same battle. The sun rises. Light overcomes darkness and the high pink clouds of morning are tinged with the blood of the snake.

I am like that cat, overcoming my own darknesses. The soul duels fear and doubt and inertia, for these are the children of the snake, the worms hidden in the clay of being that would gnaw a man to death even while he lived. I am that cat. I stand up and fight. I struggle with the evils of my own petty insistence. The battle of old gods wages in me. I am a creature of history—human and divine. I am the scroll of numerous myths, one teller of a single story.

Now the sun rises as the gold egg of god, whole light of the world, saffron cake of being. Ra shines from his disk in heaven. He rises up—a golden wonder, a bead on the throat of sky. Gusts of wind issue forth as warm breath of his mouth and drive the boats along the water, sails the sun over a river of sky and enlivens the nostrils of his people. He rises, making plain the two worlds of heaven and earth. I see myself by the light of my becoming.

8

Triumph over Darkness

EVERY SEASON OF THE FLOOD I saw god born from the buttocks of a cow. She was mighty in fullness as was the river and, likewise, the two of them struggled up toward higher ground. There upon the stony earth, the cow strained against the pain, the sharp hooves of the animal kicking inside her, even as the calf strained against the dark belly of its mother. They were warriors of a common purpose. I reached in, my hand slick and full of the primeval waters. Then, feeling bone beneath skin, I gently drew the two legs out. With a heave life was born into my hands. And the cow rested licking her calf's steaming head still wet and shining from its mother's body.

The ways of making indeed are wondrous—the child born of its mother, the sun rolling into sky, the song rising from the lips, the world springing from the word of god. The essence of life is brilliant, dazzling. I cannot explain such miracles, yet I embody them daily. Though I cannot remember my birth and shall forget my death, I live in the midst of wonder.

I stand, therefore, before myself and god, before Ra and Ptah and Osiris. I am one of those lights I see, an ember of fire climbing the back of heaven and heaven takes me in. I am its child, loved by gods.

I am a man walking the path, separating the nettles from the flowers. I am myself who perceives who I am. I am my heart's witness. I am an animal, the breath and blood of myself responding to tides, constant as sun, mutable as moon. I am a baboon driven by instinct. I am a jackal devouring the meat of life, thirsty for the stream of being. I swallow the world, I digest it, I am nourished by it. No possibility is left untasted. I am a falcon, a form of earth that rises. I am one who soars to heaven and brings home a message. I leap up from matter to ride the current of spirit.

I am a lover of truth. I cut away lies, these rags of mortality. I am incense on the altar, seven grains of moly smoldering in flame, seven sparks dancing in the air. Seven herons fly in the light of Osiris. Seven fish leap from the river into the birds' mouths. Seven stars dream in the northern sky nestled in the lap of a bear. There is a serpent writhing through heaven, unbound by the weight of earth. His tongue flicks flames. He licks the fingers of gods, but the snake left to earth licks only dark and dust.

"Come," said the lord of life to the lord of death one day. "Let us make a truce. I shall bring forth creatures and deliver them unto death, if you deliver the dead unto life."

"Why should I bequeath my powers to you?" asked death.

"It is simple enough. If you do not, I shall make no creatures at all. Then what good will your strength do you?"

"I see your point. But what good is death in the face of life, or for that matter, what good is life in the face of death?"

The two gods argued this way and that and the conversation fell upon the ears of truth. "Come now," said truth, for he was the great uniter and wanted also to show his power. "Surely there is a way to settle this matter. You, god of life, shall make two of all your creatures, one visible and the other invisible. Death may take them, but he must keep only one. The body shall be his to do with as he pleases. The spirit he shall return to life."

And so it was done that the world would remain constant in balance. They embraced one another and became one body of god. These are life and death. These are two eyes of Ra, one offering light and one burning up flesh.

On the day I saw Ra born from the buttocks of a cow I was overcome with weeping. How young was the calf, its life spread out before it. How close to death was the old cow, its mother. And I saw two worlds move closer together, the hand of one god passing a soul into the hand of the other. Was the mystery one of joy or sorrow?

Many days passed since the day I fell from the womb. Already I am old and know more men dead now than alive. The calf born that day is many years gone. I gaze into the depths of the Nile. By what shall I gauge eternity? Does the river flow on with the same water? At night I dream the heavens are full of bodies, lights and shadows, the souls of men and women returning.

These are the manifestations of Horus, a thousand thousand souls in his train, an army marching against darkness. These are souls returning to earth, men and women beatified. One spirit veiled in flesh may stand upright, white as tusks. One swirls in ether, total substance of gods. One sails through Egypt propelled by the breath of fire. One counts the wheat grains like the gods' endless hours. One weaves the cloth of dreams that clothe his brothers. One walks by day and watches by night. A thousand forms are the souls of Horus who set up lights in the darkness, who heal the sick, who write the books, who build the temples, who raise the children, who feed the people, who push the plow, who dance under stars, who dream of holy dreams. The words of power were conferred on them in Amentet that they might become the backbone of heaven.

Therefore with regularity, the spirit returns to its source to bask in the wonders of god, to draw strength from the fire, then go into the world to rage against the serpent of darkness. Therefore, the gods together are one. Therefore, I am the double soul of gods. I am priest of my own becoming, of the holiness of change, of the ways of Osiris and of Ra—a spirit of glory as the hawk, a spirit of strength as the ram. I am a light, a fire, a purpose, a rager against oblivion.

As the forms of light are numerous, so are the forms of darkness. The shapes of good and evil are hidden. I discern the fruit from the poison. In the house of death there waits a being of darkness whose eyebrows swim on his forehead like fishes. There is one of light whose two arms are the scales. One goddess recounts a man's history on the night of reckoning. The tongue of another burns rotten meat in its fire. There is the knife that would sunder what a man brings together. There is the knife that would cut away filth. There are clothes of light and skins of darkness. There are two snakes asleep in dark waters. One rises up with the head of man speaking. One rises up with two heads—one full of honor, the other full of deceit. The first snake is evil, easy enough to recognize. The second snake is the good son Horus, avenger of his father, soldier of truth. To those who tell lies, he confounds them with lies. To those who speak truths, Horus speaks truth. He is the passageway into the forms both golden and terrible.

May I know the truth when I see it. May I stand on the lotus, a son of god, and rise like perfume unto the god's nostrils. May my fingernails turn into thorns to drive back the snake. May my arms become spears to thwart crocodiles. May the light of my soul detect shadows of evil. May I listen to the voice of the messenger. May I walk the road envisioned by Ra's eyes. May my spirit gather my selves and fly back to its source. May I join the great march of beings who live and die in the circle of light.

I shall not fall under flashing knives. I shall not burn up in the cauldron. I know the names of the scorpions and they are these: anger, bitterness and doubt. And I know the names of the serpents: ego, concern for the self of the body; relinquishment of destiny, the attribution of suffering to god; false pity that stifles another man's becoming; mediocre virtues and the denial of passion; sentimentality wherein passion is artifice; satisfaction wherein he fails to attain the great; common thought wherein a man seeks not to push himself beyond the limits of his own imagination.

I am he who walks around heaven breathing the hot flame of the mouth of he who circles the edges of heaven making himself invisible, commanding the inundation of the Nile, commanding the spirits of his people. I am radiant on earth. I am a warrior of light. I burn musk and moly on the altar. I come forth from green fields. I roll gold into life like a beetle. I soar like a hawk. I squawk like a goose. I snatch green snakes with my teeth. I am the flowering branch of almond on the obsidian altar.

I am the two eyes of god creating. I live in the forehead of god dreaming. I am an old man welcomed into heaven. I am the flow and nature of things. I am forever—god's life on earth. The gifts of gods are mine: health and power and eternity.

I have seen the face of evil—one with sharp teeth like a ravaging dog that feasts upon corpses, that swallows hearts, that vomits and shoots filth from under its tail. I have seen his face, but he has not seen himself. His name is eater of millions, envy, jealousy, greed and lust. He is the robber of hours, the passion out of control that devours life without tasting it, without being nourished by it. Then he is born seven times into a place where nothing grows.

I have seen the face of evil—one with a hundred coils in its tail that would claim for itself whatever it touched: the perfume of hibiscus, the heart of a lover, the light of its days, the thoughts and passions of others. It would clutch these things, squeeze them and suck out their vitality. Then the snake would rise up with a shake of its tail and name itself god, knower of all, possessed of all wisdom. "I alone," it cries, "know the truth and I shall keep it." He is the serpent that separates men from gods.

I have seen the face of evil—a face full of burns and scars, tortures inflicted upon the self. He would scald his own chest and blame it on others. He would slash his own wrists and blame it on the gods. He is the blamer, the finder of fault. He is author of all the ill that befalls him, unrepentant and unconscious. Blind is he even to the motion of his own hand that rises up and plucks out his eyes.

Who then shall guard us from these terrors? We ourselves and the beating heart of Osiris and the bones of his back that make us rise up in truth. We shall walk with him around the edge of the Lake of Fire. We shall possess the loves, the words, the bodies we know. We shall walk glorious in Egypt, our hearts swelling with passion, our lungs filled with the breath of fire, all the gods and goddesses united in one body. Now is the day of the joining of opposites, of the mingling of the dust of flesh with the dust of the coffin. This is the day of flow, the living ether returned to air, the maker of forms assuming new form. This is the day without end—the passage into light itself, the joining of Osiris to Ra.

I have seen the face of justice, the terrible face of Osiris who is generator of spirit and degenerator of matter, whose tongue of fire licks away flesh, whose mouth devours filth, who stands before darkness as a guardian of light. Oh evil ones, fall down and shiver for he who lives truth passes by him, but he who lives lies falls, is held fast in his nets, is seized in his jaws. He is messenger of light, bestower of life and taker away. This white boat of spirit ferries the body through dark waters, carries the heart of gold through the red core of earth. Great is the god in his boat. Great are the ways of becoming, the change-and-change again, the cycle of truth in the body. Great is the dough of life, malleable god-stuff from which earth and heaven are made.

I have seen the face of justice, the beatific face of Osiris, the whisperer of truth in the darkness, the power of moving on past mortality and illusion. No great evil comes to he who breathes the breath of his nostrils, who follows the path of the lightning flash that leaps to form between the two worlds.

I am a traveler on the way, pure of heart. I am a son fresh from his birth. I have eaten the gods' saffron cakes laid out on platters of blue faience. I was given the bread of Osiris in the house of feasting. I saw the changes in myself, the god in his body, the beauty in earth, the gold orb of the sky making the corn green in the fields. Those who speak the words of becoming are the goddesses of dream and intuition, the magic of earth speaking beneath a brilliant sky under a carpet of unfolding yellow flowers. I am he who ate the saffron cakes.

I've known the pleasures of the earth. I bathed myself in light on an afternoon of rejoicing—not a festival, but an ordinary afternoon where I opened my heart to the world and the world came in, where I brought water from the well with my daughter, where I chewed the grass, ate the figs and sat by the riverbank watching sunlight dazzle like the white pearls of my daughter's smile. I steeped myself in the passion for existence until my spirit rose like steam bearing the fragrance of cedar and flowers. I brought offerings to the gods: belladonna and mandrake and wine. I brought moly and frankincense, visions of peace unending. I brought turquoise and silver and carnelian, the stone of earth's joyful singing. I brought the earth ground into the pores of my skin and the melons I grew by the river. I brought yesterday and today and the sun rising between them, the roar of wind and time like two lions. I brought only those things which Ptah had made, which I cared for and give back. I bring home the earth. I bring back the words.

There are days when a man must take up the sword and days when he puts it away. For now, at this moment, I am done with darkness. Blessed is the world of Ptah. Blessed is the world fashioned by his hands. Blessed is the word of Atum's mouth. I am a lotus rising up, my thousand petals of existence.

I am watched over by goddesses as Isis concealed her husband in her curtain of hair, as she veiled his body in light. The fragrance of her perfume falls over me—her hair! I am under its spell, drunk with love, entwined in arms of splendor, born in magic, engendered in dream, caught up in the whirl of existence. The weight of the heart is severed from me. I am drifting off, spinning, burning, waxing, waning . . . I am taking form. I am embraced in her thighs a million years. I am the body of her lover, full of awe and passion. And the mortals spin round and round beside me. I am refreshed. I come into being.

Now I seize darkness by its arms and shake it. The souls of ancient swallowed gods fall out of the belly of obscurity. The old, the few and the forgotten walk back into being with me. I am bringing home the world. I am triumphant. My wife kisses me twice. I bring to form the man I am, the thoughts I imagined, the worlds I dreamed. The bones of my head burst into flame. I shoot fiery arrows into night's darkness and they are like falling stars, messages of light. I live according to what I know and love, the healing of words, the healing of herbs, the stealing of kisses, the pleasures and duties of men.

I live in the eye of the lady of flame. I am light reflected by Hathor's mirror. The words of goddesses are bright and shining in my mouth. I create myself. I am the gods' secret. I have seen the great fire of perhaps, the beacon of possibility. I wake in the liquid light of a vision. Now Isis stands up and combs back her hair.

9

Seven Houses in the Other World

I COME TO THE STONY hidden place in a valley circled by mountains, a world grown apart from the bright green land I knew, but like it, in the shape of that memory. I round a corner that seems to leap, to speak of a sudden day I passed fifty-two years ago in the crook of a tree in my grandfather's orchard. In a few more steps, I'll be there with them—the old man and a few of his sons, my father and uncles flinging their whips lightly across the backsides of the donkeys. The smell of grapes, pomegranates and figs already intoxicates me.

But no, I am mistaken. There are no trees, only this stone wall, old and already crumbling, which divides the man from the boy he was. Darkness lies thick with forgetfulness on this side of the wall and that. I look back. The straight road behind me changes. It twists and twines beneath a night without stars. Is it even the same road I travelled a moment ago? Before my eyes, it writhes and twists yet again. One hill looms ahead; one grows behind. I am deep in a valley, the unfamiliar ground cold and sunless. I walk twisting paths. I go round in coils of earth. I travel the back of a snake.

I come to the first house of challenge. Three gods dream inside the doorway. One bears the head of a crocodile. One holds an ear of corn. Power and life they are and between them rises the last—tall and poised as a cobra, straight as a pillar of stone. I cry out: "You, doorkeeper, upside down face! You, creature of many forms! You, watchman, with the eyes and ears of creation! You, herald, with the piercing wail! Let me pass! Let me pass! Let the memory of an old man pass! I am a mighty one, too. I am a spirit walking in darkness by the light of his own divinity. I have come. I have cut loose my body. I am a worshipper of light. Lead on. Show me the ways of change, the roads that lead through the twisting gut of the mountain. Bless you, mighty gods, for the powers that guide me. I have risen up and walked about in heaven. I have been raised up like a pillar of light. I have sailed with Ra in the boat of the sun. Bless him in his spinning round the circuit of sky. I have come to the place of the eye, the ground where common men reap good or ill harvests. I am precious as a stalk of wheat. I am the unbroken seal on the book of myself. I have made my changes. I am a being of becomings. Open the way to me. Let me pass through the wall of misconception. Let me walk burning coals. I shall ease the pain and sorrow of gods with the sweet pods of carob trees, with the fragrant perfume of memory, with the pungent odor of love. My words are heartfelt, my herbs powerful as any priest's, my prayers like incense to the nostrils of gods. I am a soul longing for greatness, walking a dark road on the way to becoming. I have cut a path from here through the mountain and my spirit flares with the fire of god. I am a shining, recollected Osiris. My face is aglow with white heat."

Then the doors open. I pass through and the doors shut, then the house vanishes in the night behind me. The straight road twists and twines behind me beneath a night without stars. I walk on unfamiliar ground. I travel the back of a snake.

I come to the second house of challenge. Three gods conspire inside the doorway. One roars with the jaws of a lion. Two figures flash knives. I cry out: "You, doorkeeper, first being uttered from Atum's teeth! You, watchman, dog-faced pylon! You, herald, with the bloody flint of a knife! Let me pass! Let me pass! Let the body of an old man pass! Oh what joy it was once to be young! When all a man had to do was eat and sweat and make love to his wife. But that was not even the height of my powers. I learned more or less in time to weigh my words, to conserve my actions, even at last to suppress my little will, ah! but never to deny my feelings. Love and anger gave me words of truth, but I refined them and I was no less a man of passion for my caution. The virtues of Thoth made of me more god. I gave the mind the pleasure of creation. I sought out the truth, though difficult and hidden. And the strength of Osiris was the strength of the mind, the strength of the hand, the strength of will and god. I am heavy as stone, not easily blown by the breezes, but I sail when I must and strike a blow to untruth. I offer myself in this moment, a man in the dark walking by his own light along the way. I pass on. I am a priest of light, a man of conviction. I have risen up and walked about in heaven. I have made my changes. I am a being of becomings. Open the way to me. Lead me on the road gnarled as serpents. Show me the ways that lead through the twisting gut of the mountain that I might find Ra at last and grasp him like the water skin, that these parched old lips might quench their thirst with the cool white liquid of light."

Then the doors open. I pass through and the doors shut, then the house vanishes in the night behind me. The straight road twists and twines behind me beneath a night without stars. I walk unfamiliar ground. I travel the back of a snake, or else the snake's intestines.

I come to the third house of challenge. Three gods dance in the doorway. Two wear the sharp snouts of the jackal. One serpent spins round and round about a stalk of corn. I cry out: "You, doorkeeper, gobbler of your own shit! You, watchman, uplifting your face! I am not afraid of your obsidian eye. You, herald, oh great voice of thunder! Let me pass! Let me pass! Let the shadow of an old man pass! I am hidden in the deep. I am a form in the green ocean of being. I am a thought sprung from the forehead of god. I am one of many. I, myself, am secret and following secret ways, the paths of which are unknown to me. I have cast out sadness. I have thrown down fear. I leap in the air and snatch the yellow ribbons of day. I have done what the gods willed for me. I molded my body in clay on the potter's wheel. I carved my own heart out of carnelian and gave to my family my red, red love. In all my thoughts I chiseled the gods' names and the words of power were set into stone. Light leaps from the top of my head toward heaven. Light leaps up like the two white horns of a bull. I walk this road in the other world, a passage curled and nebulous as smoke. I ease the pain of becoming, the sorrow of gods with the sweet pods of the carob. My heart has been weighed in the balance. I walk the paths of gods. I am a light shining in the darkness. Let me pass. Show me the ways that lead on through the twisting gut of the mountain."

Then the doors open. I pass through and the doors shut, then the house vanishes in the night behind me. The straight road twists and twines behind me beneath a night without stars. I walk unfamiliar ground. I travel the back of a snake.

I come to the fourth house of challenge. Three gods shimmer in the doorway. One is a golden hawk soaring. One beast wears the face of a man. One man wears the face of a lion. I cry out: "You, doorkeeper, great of speech but repulsive of face! You, watchman, who sees what lies ahead! You, herald, repulser of the crocodile! Let me pass! Let me pass! Let the beating heart of an old man pass! I am a spirit. I am an ox. I am the power of generation, the making of myself, the son of limitless earth and sky. I am the heart of Osiris, pillar of my mother's house, light of my father. I am a scribe faithful to the language of the heart. I am a man born under fortunate stars into the hands of gods and goddesses. I have cut loose my body. I have risen up and walked about heaven. I have judged the guilt in my own heart, cut out its defects and burned them in fire. The air in my nose is the breath of gods, the fragrance of lotus, the life eternal, the breeze that bends the willing wheat. I rise from the egg of the world. I am a son of earth. Let me pass. Open the ways through the twisting gut of the mountain. I cross the river into this other world. I am light sailing on air. I have cut loose my body."

Then the doors open. I pass through and the doors shut, then the house vanishes in the night behind me. The straight road twists and twines behind me beneath a night without stars. I walk unfamiliar ground. I follow the ribbon of a snake.

I come to the fifth house of challenge. Three gods guard the doorway. Each holds a knife. One sprouts the wings and beak of a hawk. One has the head of seven writhing snakes. I cry out: "You, doorkeeper, groveling in the dirt, living on worms! You, watchman, you pool of fire! You, herald, with the hippo face, falling down before god! Let me pass! Let me pass! Let the name of an old man pass! I travelled the ways of change, roads that twist through the bowels of the mountain. I have brought my jawbones. I have carried the bones of my skull and back that I might recollect myself, that I might become a pillar of heaven, a watchtower, a light unto the world. I have gathered my opposites, my fragmented thoughts, desires and flesh. I walk by the light of my divinity. I am the thousand sparks of fire returning, becoming one with flame. I have taken the wax image of the snake, cut it with a knife and spat on its wounds. I have thrown evil into the fire and evil was burned away. I, too, am a warrior, a light among you. I walk the winding, secret paths in the mountain. I am an old man, an old soul, ancient among gods. I poured the oils of lemons and hibiscus over my white hair. I made my body fragrant that goddesses might come and kiss me, make me rise with life, tough and strong as a cow's horn. Open the way. I am a man already victorious having come through a long night. I gathered myself, my bones, my images and reflections, all the names I have called myself. I have saved from the crocodile my pieces of flesh, the countless lives I have lived, the comfortless loves I once savored. Let me pass on. Grant me passion along the way that I may complete my becoming."

Then the doors open. I pass through and the doors shut, then the house vanishes in the night behind me. The straight road twists on beneath a night without stars. I walk unfamiliar ground. I travel the long back of a snake.

I come to the sixth house of challenge. Three gods sleep inside the doorway, three dogs, three tongues lolling, three bellies drunk with meat. I cry out: "You, doorkeeper, with sharp and terrible teeth! You, watchman, hunter of great triumph! You, herald, who snaps at the heels of anyone who tries to scale these walls! Let me pass! Let me pass! Let the light of an old man pass! I have come like the sun bursting forth on the first day. I am radiant as the light of morning—constant and full of renewal. I have kept my eye on the path, the winding secret ways through the mountain. I am a light approaching the end of night. I have left behind what was made of nature, the body of earth, the clay, the water. I am a body new in spirit. I carry the crown of existence, the man I became I became without the aid of magic, but through will and devotion and action, through determination to walk in truth with light. I have seen the great world and the small one. I gave my sight to the gods and the gods gave me visions. I walked a dark road by the light of the eye in my forehead, the insight, the illumination. I am a creature of light walking with god. Let me pass over into heaven. Let me pass for my journey is nearly complete. It is not the end of the path, but its source, the beginning. I walk on in the heart of god."

Then the doors open. I pass through and the doors shut, then the house vanishes in the night behind me. The road twists and curls and twines. The road rears up. It is the head of the snake, and I walk the path of its crooked flickering tongue. I pass the two obelisks of its teeth. I walk in a night on fire with stars.

I come to the seventh house of challenge. Three gods lock hands inside the doorway. The lion and the hare cross lances against me. But the old man between the guardians smiles. He resembles me. His two hands hold ears of corn. I cry out: "You, doorkeeper, with sharp, slashing knife! You, watchman, carrying my own face! You, herald, with words sharp as a knife! Let me pass! Let me pass! Let the marrow of an old man pass! I have come home bringing my soul. I am Osiris, pure in emanation, clothed in oils and linen. I have cut loose my body. I walk about stars. I sail the heavens with gods. I hold long conversations with beings of light. I am a mind afire. I am the sun from noon to dusk, heat of the day, blaze of sunset. I am I—the only one like me in all the universe, my memories unique, my thoughts colored by my loves, my body built of the bread my teeth have ground. I walk round the shining house of heaven. I speak of the things on earth that I loved, the orchard of my grandfather, the song of my mother, my daughter kneading bread, the lips and hair of my wife, the downy cheeks of my grandchildren, the hawks that soared by the cliffs near my field. I speak of things of matter, the life that possessed this body, and though I pass away, these things do not but live in me. I carry into heaven the life of earth. From the stuff of forms I gained words enough to speak of myself. I am I—an old man become strong, a tongue spitting light into darkness."

Then the doors open. I pass through and the doors shut, then the house vanishes in the night behind me. The road rises and falls. Ahead lies a path, a gold and silver river sparkling in dawn's light. Bones grow out of the ether of my fingers. Soft, pink flesh curls around me. My head grows a jungle of thick black hair. I change. I grow into existence. I turn back. The straight road behind me changes. It twists and twines between rows of date palms, olives and grape arbors. Is it even the same road I travelled a moment ago? I walk on earth again in the light—or is it heaven, another circular path? I change and change again. I am a god and the ways lie open, all the paths of my various becomings. The air in my nose smells sweet. My heart swells with joy. I walk on twisting paths across new ground. My legs are strong. The journey ahead stays uncertain. I am the essence of what I am, travelling the back of a snake.

10

Twenty-One
Women

THE HEART OF THE WORLD is crystal marked by twenty-one paths and one narrow road, thin as a flint blade, that the fool walks. The ways of goddesses are devious. Temples fill with temptresses, dark-skinned dancers, daughters, mothers. A man walks alone by his own light.

He comes to the first pylon. He speaks. Lady of terror, whose heart is a wall, mistress of destruction. Lady of alarm, ruin and despair, too-wise bird of no good omen. Priestess and dancer whose words are fires that crackle and spit in a man's face. Lady of rage, she creates nightmares by the thousands. She spins. With a black word she drives back the serpent and the traveler goes on his way. Her name is "Vulture Mother of Terror." Blessed is the lady.

He comes to the second pylon. Lady of heaven, cup of flame, courtesan of two worlds, whore of heaven, mother of mortals. Hers is the body of love, milky paps and flesh so vast a man gets lost. She, the lover of every man, every woman, every beast. She, the mistress of no one. She devours all in the flame of her lioness mouth. Her name is "Daughter of Ptah." Blessed is the lady.

He comes to the third pylon. Lady of the altar, lady of the lotus, great pool of emotion and memory. Two eyes of the world to whom offerings of myrrh are made, she is a heap of dream. She is the flower bursting forth. She is desire, beloved of every god. She is the pleasure and all gods unite with her. Her name is "Noble Sycamore." Blessed is the lady.

He comes to the fourth pylon. Lady of the knife slashing, bits of flesh in her hair. Lady dancing on earth, vessel of the world. She cuts the throats of her enemies. She uplifts the weary man. Her heart is slight as a feather. She fills the void within with courage. She feeds him, she clothes him, she throws open the door to forever. She provides his escape on the back of a cow. Her name is "Ponderous Bull." Blessed is the lady.

He comes to the fifth pylon. Flame, flame. Lady of breath, fragrant woman of air, whose words are hot and sweet in his nostrils. No man may come to her. No man may sleep exhausted on her breast. No man may beseech her aloud. No man may stand before her presence. She is eternity, essence, window onto forever. Her name is "Moment of the Flood." Blessed is the lady.

He comes to the sixth pylon. Lady of light, warm, round, sun-darkened breast. Lady of might for whom men wail and shout. Lady of love, bond of woman to son. None know her height, nor breadth, nor magnitude. No creature ever was fashioned like her. No sorrow was known as deep as the sorrow of those who suckled her. No man or woman ever rose from her arms. She encompasses all. Beneath her robe curls a worm in an empty sky. Turn back, faint of heart, or lie stillborn in her forever. Her name is "Companion of Death." Blessed is the lady.

He comes to the seventh pylon. Lady of tatters, rags and cloth. Mistress of the robe, clothier of the dead, woman who weeps and hides her weeping. She is widow, concealer, sorceress. She is dew and rain and tears. She sobs into the shroud of the man she loves. He lies still and hears her weeping. What she loves remains secret. Her name is "Beauty." Blessed is the lady.

He comes to the eighth pylon. Lady of the pyre, fire blazing, whose flame never dies. Lady of the heat, she burns up transgression. Her flame is sharp, her fingers are orange spikes. She speaks with a tongue of far-reaching fire. Her hands are quick. She burns flesh into ash and light. None may pass by or through her without risking death. She is the necessity, justice, awesome power. Her name is "Flame That Protects His Body." Blessed is the lady.

He comes to the ninth pylon. Lady of the forearm, lady of strength, lady who dwells with snakes. Lady who opens the lion's mouth, who soothes the souls of her priests with her bread. Lady of wisdom and pleasure. She measures the year that travels her girth. She is the tree and its branches. She is the cycle of gods, the aura of light, the river, the field of emerald and turquoise. She is the face of every woman in love, the strength of those who enter her. Her name is "Eye of Her Own Song." Blessed is the lady.

He comes to the tenth pylon. Lady of thunder whose voice is a roar, who rattles the teeth of men. Lady of the wheel, of the fates, of the fist. Lady of high, terrible laughter. Lady of jubilation in the face of the vulture. She makes men howl in her clamorous presence. She fears no man on earth or beneath. Her name is "Priestess of Heaven." Blessed is the lady.

He comes to the eleventh pylon. Lady of the repeated slaughter, beastly lady who stamps her hooves, who brands fiends and rebels, most terrible lady of all. A serpent has crawled round her heart. She rejoices on the day of darkness. She stands guard before the gate. She pierces a man with the flame of her eye. She weighs his life in her palm. She speaks not, inquires not. In silence she interrogates a man's soul. Her name is not known. Blessed is the lady.

He comes to the twelfth pylon. Lady of splendor, mistress of two worlds, invoking the powers of both. She commands her soldiers into battle. She chars her enemies with fire. She is the magnificent rising sun, radiant, bright light of the world. She is the gold orb thrust above the hill, sparkle of cosmic mind, god embedded in self. In the midst of her dance she stops, hears the voice of her lord. She speaks not his name, inquires not. In silence she interrogates his soul. Her name is not known. Blessed is the lady.

He comes to the thirteenth pylon. Death. Death. Eternity. Lady Isis gathers his bones together. She marries him unto the grave. She reaches down and draws him up in her two arms. She stretches her hands over his stinking flesh. She causes the waters to ripple, the Nile to rise, the evening star to shine. She awaits his embrace. His face is aglow with white heat. "Magic and Marriage," "Love and Dissolve" are her names. Blessed is the lady.

He comes to the fourteenth pylon. Lady of the knife, dancing on blood, red dancer, flamingo woman. Hers are the flowers in decay, the columns of the temples pulled down, the intrigue of beauty that lies in ruin. Her hands separate the dead from the spirits of the dead. Hers is the hour of hearing catastrophes. In silence she interrogates his soul. Her name is not known. Blessed is the lady.

He comes to the fifteenth pylon. Lady of scrutiny, lady of carnelian souls. She finds reason to make a man miserable. She finds reason to cause a man to scream. She binds him with a cry. With a shout she holds him fast. Her knife slashes through his intestines. She speaks not his name, inquires not. In silence she interrogates his soul. Her name is not known. Blessed is the lady.

He comes to the sixteenth pylon. Lady of the rainstorm, lady of the eye, hastener of the lotus blossoms. She tastes the flesh of dead men, her breath withers the flowers, her red eye foretells the future. She bursts forth, the teeth of a lioness, the power of nature in her belly, the lust for blood. She is the self studying the self. She speaks not his name, inquires not. In silence she interrogates his soul. Her name is not known. Blessed is the lady.

He comes to the seventeenth pylon. A star trembles in the sky. Lady of diminished returns, hacker to pieces, lessener, subtracter, divider. She burns his flesh above a candle. Lady of flame, she binds him in rags. Lady of myrrh and frankincense, she fills his nostrils with herbs. She speaks not his name, inquires not. In silence she interrogates his soul. Her name is not known. Blessed is the lady.

He comes to the eighteenth pylon. Lady of the temple, lover of fire, purifier of sinners. She is heat. She is mother of the whetstone and knife. She lusts for mutilation, for the heads of those who love her. Lady of the temple, the palace, the slaughterhouse. She smells the blood in her nose. She is the back of the head, the eternal dream. She speaks not his name, inquires not. In silence she interrogates his soul. Her name is not known. Blessed is the lady.

He comes to the nineteenth pylon. Old woman whose teeth are broken and brown. Lady of dusk who was once the song bird. She was early light, the rattling seeds of the sistrum, a brilliant moment in time. She spends her days as mistress of flames. Lady of endurance, lady of strength. She holds the power over his mouth. She chants the songs of goddesses. She reads the library of a man's life. She speaks not his name, inquires not. In silence she interrogates his soul. Her name is not known. Blessed is the lady.

He comes to the twentieth pylon. Lady of the tomb, lady of the mastaba, lady of the cavern. She is the resurrection. She is the sanctuary, the rock in the side of the mountain. She is the wall, the veil, the mask, the sorceress who hides her creations. She carries away the faint of heart. She devours the bread of the corpse, the wine of blood. Her name is "Concealer." In silence she interrogates his soul. Blessed is the lady.

He comes to the twenty-first pylon. Lady of the universe, lady of crossed destinies, lady of vibrations. She is the name of a man when first it is uttered. She molds his form in wax and tosses it to flames. She brings secret paths. She possesses hidden schemes. She plots a man's life in accordance with divine will. Her name is not known. Her power is greatest. Blessed is the lady.

I am a man whose heart is pure, who walked the paths of darkness, who shone in the houses of the other world, who came back to heaven and on earth bearing light. I passed the mothers, the daughters and the grandmothers of vultures. I have seen the underside of beauty. I have gazed long in Hathor's mirror and seen the hidden faces of goddesses. And I shall go on believing in light, for only light and love denied can make the faces of women so terrible.

11

Triumph through the Cities

HAIL THOTH, ARCHITECT OF TRUTH, give me words of power that I may write the story of my own becoming. I stand before the masters who witnessed the creation, who were with Ra that morning the sun rolled into being, who were with Osiris in the grave as he gathered himself together and burst from the tomb white with heat, a light and shining god. And they are Atum, who uttered the word of beginning, and his children, mist and air. I, too, am a man longing for unity. I, too, am a man who holds the lance of light, who strikes a blow against darkness as when Ra appears at dawn and sends his sword into the belly of night and the serpent spews back all the things he has swallowed. I wait to come forth by day in Heliopolis, city of light.

Hail Thoth, architect of truth, give me words of power that I may recall the years and weave together my history. I stand before the masters who witnessed the recollection of Osiris, who gathered together his backbones, who set up columns of carnelian and gold, who built around themselves a fortress of strength with the lapis lazuli of god. And they are Osiris, whose body was severed, Isis and Nephthys, who gathered his parts, and Horus, who avenged his death by striking a blow against evil. He raised him up in deed and memory. He wound the cloth of being tight and, retelling his father's history, became the shoulder whereon Osiris stood. Then the goddesses sailed upon the Nile in boats of twinkling lights, one for each day to mark the year that Osiris was king. I, too, am a man longing for unity. I wait to come forth strong in Tettu, fortress of the god's backbones.

Hail Thoth, architect of truth, give me words of power that I may form the characters of my own evolution. I stand before the masters who witnessed the genesis, who were the authors of their own forms, who rolled into being, who walked the dark circuitous passages of their own becoming, who saw with their own eyes their destinies and the shapes of things to come. And they are Thoth, the beetle Khepera, and Horus, the child become man. I, too, am a man longing for change. I wait to come forth by day in Sekhem, city of unified forms.

Hail Thoth, architect of truth, give me words of power that I may envision the course of events that a life must follow. I stand before the masters who attended the birth of Horus, who at his conception decreed on him the duty to avenge his father, who hid the child and his mother in the papyrus swamps, who shielded the infant in obscurity that he might grow in secret, who commanded the dreams wherein his father spoke of his future destiny. And they are Horus himself and Isis, who conceived him in magic, and Mestha, who was the spirit's witness, and Hapi, the voice of the Nile which taught the child flux and flow. I, too, am a man longing to attend destiny. I sit in silence listening to the lady of flame, that flickering tongue of the inner voice, the conscience, the self-prophecy. I wait to come forth by day in Pe-tep, cities of obscurity.

Hail Thoth, architect of truth, give me words of power that I may intuit the symbols of dream and command my own becoming. I stand before the masters who witnessed the working of magic, who were with Isis the evening she became the swallow and her lamentations filled the air, who were with her as she shook down her black hair and veiled the god's transformation in secret, who witnessed the conception of the divine child though his coming was yet unrevealed. And they are Isis, who worked the charm, and Hathor, who interpreted the stars. And they are goddesses of beauty and of wonder and of revelation. I, too, am a man who dreams. I, too, believe in miracles and I work my spells well to achieve them. I wait to come forth by day in Sept, city of shredding the veil.

Hail Thoth, architect of truth, give me words of power that when I speak the life of a man I may give his story meaning. I stand before the masters who know the histories of the dead, who decide which tales to hear again, who judge the books of lives as either full or empty, who are themselves authors of truth. And they are Isis and Osiris, the divine intelligences. And when the story is written and the end is good and the soul of a man is perfected, with a shout they lift him into heaven. I, too, am a man longing for perfection. I wait to shine forth in Manu, the place of the setting sun.

Hail Thoth, architect of truth, give me words of power that I may tell the truth of my own becoming. I stand before the masters who witness the judgment of souls, who sniff out the misdeeds, the imperfections, the lies and half-truths we tell ourselves in the dark. And they are Thoth and his two companions, Anubis and Asten, who hold the books of truths and lies and make comparisons. It is the night of blotting out souls, of staying transformation, of withholding the power of a man to make mischief. Speak. I am a man longing for candor. I wait to come forth by day in Abydos, city of the dead.

Hail Thoth, architect of truth, give me words of power that I may complete my story and begin life anew. I stand before the masters who witnessed the plowing of earth, who saw the seed that entered the fields spring into corn and barley, who sent the flood and sun, who saw men among the wheat swinging scythes, who saw women baking bread. And the death of the wheat was not lost. And a new beginning was foretold in the end that a man may rise from his grave singing. And the divine witnesses are the souls of animals; the souls of wheat, vegetables and men; the souls of everything that heaven and earth created and the souls of everything they shall claim again. So the river of life is red as blood and light as the breath of spirit. I wait to come forth again in Sekhet-Aaru, the greening fields of papyrus.

Hail Thoth, architect of truth, give me words of power that I may create myself from my dreams of becoming. I stand before the masters who witnessed the transformation of the body of a man into the body in spirit, who were witnesses to resurrection when the corpse of Osiris entered the mountain and the soul of Osiris walked out shining. And they are Ra, the light of divinity, and Shu, the breath of god. He gathered his thigh, his heel and his leg. He gathered his arms and backbones. He gathered the dreams crackling inside the dark cave of his skull. He knitted himself together in secret. He came forth from death, a shining thing, his face white with heat. I, too, am a man longing for unity. I wait at the passageway into the mountain. I come forth by day to Anrutf, doorway to transformation.

Hail Thoth, architect of truth, give me words of power that the heart of my story may beat strong enough for a man to rise up and walk in it. I stand before the masters who witnessed the magic of making. And they are Horus and Isis who stood before the corpse of Osiris, but it was Anubis who spread his hands, wrenched open the chest and commanded the heart of Osiris to beat, to cleave and make way for the light that was coming. Then the will of Osiris rose up and spoke to its body. His heart beat and Isis rejoiced, then Horus was born in the body of spirit. Osiris united with heaven and earth. I, too, am a man longing for unity. I, too, am a soul opening unto light. I wait to come forth by day in Restau, the passage unto god.

Hail Thoth, architect of truth, give me words of power before gods and goddesses and creatures of light and the messengers of heaven. Grant me unity of the heart, mind and spirit. Grant me love and light, an everlasting body. Grant me the words of transformation and the will of the flesh to make things happen. I wait to come forth by day again. My body turns to greening. I wait to give birth unto dream, to give form to the peace in my heart. I shall be a man on earth shaping the things of god. I am light entering unto fire, coming forth and shining through darkness. May I walk beneath blue heaven singing, my heart telling the story of light. I am a man blessed by becoming millions and millions of times.

12

The Arrival

I HAVE COME LIKE A priest in panther skin, having crossed the Nile by boat, having come through the gap in the mountains, having walked black corridors restless. Like a rabbit from the depth of its hutch, blinking at light, I have come. In my heart a lyre is humming. Its strings ring true. My body is a rolled papyrus tied with red string that holds no pretense. I shall not see such misery and love again. I spread the length of myself before friends and gods and let them study me. What I have done needed to be done. What I said needed to be said. No malice obscures the crystal pool of my heart. No worms hide in the folds of my scroll. I have come to the other world a pure man. I am washed and fasted.

There is no rest in Egypt. The laurel tree sends forth no shoots, the oasis shrinks to sand, the fig tree gives up no fruit. Men hammer the hard heart of the mountain, but the mountain refuses them gold. They grow weary and turn wicked. Yet I have done what must be done. I led seven goats to the temple. I offered cake to the gods. When I spoke, butterflies burst from the crevices of my lips. I burned three grains of moly every day. I brought my father oxen and ducks. I fed the hungry and clothed the beggars. I gave water to the thirsty. I drove away scorpions, marauders and thieves. I've sailed the Nile and walked through the gap in the mountain. Faithful in word like a scribe I have come. I've walked darker chambers believing in light.

In return I ask for only a little honied cake and a loaf of bread heaped high in the pan. I ask to enter those houses lit by candles and gods, and to fill my nostrils with the smoke of prayer, to come and go in the dark world, to sail the Nile again. I ask for water and a strong sailing wind, and a delta island on which to raise my children, wheat and cattle.

I have come to this dark world like a bright star in the southern sky, a shaft of light gleaming in the hawk's eye.

13

Giving a Mouth
to Osiris

I RISE FROM A BURIED EGG. Give me my mouth; I want to talk. Give me iron words forged in fire that I may speak the language of earth. In the dark house I stand at the top of the stairs. I am I. I am Osiris. I have come because I wish to have come. My two hands cling like ancestors. My lips are red as ox blood. I speak charms that drive snakes back into the rocks and bring the lotus to flower. In my time I've been struck dumb by the sun. Stars fall into my heart, a pool of fire. I am a man grown weary of ignorance, consumed in darkness and light. Give me a mouth; I want to talk. I am a child of earth and sky who rose from the buried egg, who followed his heart like light following the sun into this season of fire. Give me raisin cake and beer. Bless me with ancient dreams. Give me songs green as earth.

14

Opening the Mouth
of Osiris

UNTIE THESE RAGS ON MY FACE. Open my mouth. Unbind my legs. Give me charms and incense and cake. Pry open my mouth with the red knife of heaven and I will speak of days unending.

I am a wild goose honking. I am an ember burning in the heartland of Egypt. Open my mouth and fill me with the countless lights of heaven. Bind the jaws of doomsayers and let me dance on their rotten teeth. I strain against the lies told about me as I strain against the bondage of earth. Open my mouth. Build a bright fire of rags on the west bank of the Nile. We shall roast the leg of an antelope. Give all the gods mouths to sing.

Giving Charms
to Osiris

ONE DAY THE MOVEMENT OF moon and sun had nothing to do with seasons and that day I crawled from my mother's legs. I am Osiris spawned from two thighs. In such manner wolves are made and lift their shaggy heads to howl beneath stars. In such manner hyenas call.

I remember receiving a charm, who gave it and where, how the spell held me fast as nets, quicker than greyhounds, fleeter than light. I remember the place in every man. Now bring me a boat in the wind, strong in the wind, fast in the wind. Sail it over this lake of fire, quicker than greyhounds, fleeter than light.

Look how the charm is everywhere, how it rests in the hands of men, how life creates itself as I did from my mother's thighs. Look at it as I must look at it. Its silence fills me up. It gives power to my hands, light to my feet. It fills my head with heat.

Bring me a charm, a boat in the wind, strong in the wind, quicker than greyhounds, fleeter than light.

16

Remembering
His Name

AT NIGHT IN THIS HOUSE of fire I recount the sadness of years.
I tell the story of months. Give me my name. Say it over red jasper
dipped in an unguent of flowers. When I had no visions, ravens came
for my eyes. The breath of life escaped. When I had no words, worms
crawled through my teeth. I am more than flesh and bone. I am more
than the deeds I have done. I am more than all I remember. Give me
my name. Say it over red jasper laid in the heart of sycamore. Give me my
name that gods may call me to soar like the hawk and crane.

Giving a Heart to Osiris

MY HEART SLEEPS IN THE house of hearts. My heart dreams in the house of hearts. It does not rest with me. It does not rest in the palm of my hand. On the east bank of the river, I am too sad to eat cake. White lilies float by on green water. A boat goes down the Nile. It comes back, having ferried another man to his tomb under the rocks. It hoists its sail for me.

I can't go. I haven't the heart.

Give me a mouth. I want to talk. Give me my severed legs and I'll walk. Give me hands and arms and fists and I'll shout and curse. I'll crush the skull of the snake. Throw open the door of heaven. Perhaps Ra has two jawbones to give me. He'll open my blind eyes, straighten my bent feet. He'll give me legs and I'll rise. I'll rise. By heaven I'll walk. I know my heart. It stirs within me. It throbs in my right hand. Blood quickens beneath my skin.

Give me my heart. Let it pump again life's power in me, infuse my hands and feet with spirit. Give me my heart. Let me rise and walk. I am quickened. No more sleep. No more dream. No more death.

18

Giving Breath to Osiris

I AM THE BLUE EGG of the Great Cackler. I am the egg of the world. I was asleep inside a mound of dirt, now I rise from a buried egg. I live, I say; I live. I smell the air. I sniff the air. I walk with my toes in black earth. I give my family duck-meat to eat. I guard the fledgling in the nest. What food there is for man in the sky, blue sky. A swallow darts and circles. I am the egg. I smell the air.

I am the first-born, the light of the sky. I breathe in the presence of gods under the belly of sky, upon the shoulder of Egypt. My breath is like a child to me. My breath hangs sweet in my nostrils. I am the blue egg of the Great Cackler. I grow, I swell, I sniff the air. I live there like the wing of a goose.

What a journey I have made, what things I have seen. I am one of you. In my hand I grasp the sailing mast while my left hand trails in the water. The trees are heavy with figs and olives. The dates drop to the ground. I have separated myself from myself to sail the green Nile again. I sail to the temple where gods have gathered to gaze at their faces in deep pools. In my boat the souls of the years sail with me. The hair stands on my head in the wind. I hear the splashing of oars like the cracking of a thin, blue shell. My son keeps one hand on the rudder. What a journey we have made, what things we have seen. We glide to the middle of the lake. The hippo raises herself and smiles. Give me a cup of milk and cake and bread. Give me a jug of water and the comfort of flesh. Give me air to breathe and a strong sailing wind and I shall rise, sail out of the dark world, be blown by the warm breath of god.

A sycamore rises white from the river, filling itself with water and air. Fill me with water and air. I am the blue egg of the Great Cackler and I sniff the breezes. I grow, I live, I breathe and live. On the banks of the Nile the sky fills with birds and the sails of boats swell like lungs.

Drinking Water

I AM HE WHOSE FEET are dusty. I am a man like any man born from a blue egg buried. I've seen the flood above the cypress and known the power within. I've swung wide the two blue doors of heaven. Green water swings wide at the bow of my boat. I've sailed the waterways of the Nile and entered the sea of heaven. Give me water to drink. Quench my thirst. Give me the power of water.

I have rubbed shoulders with those who've rubbed shoulders with Ra. I have envisioned angels without ceasing. I've dreamed the white heat of my own resurrection. I've passed through the floods of emotion and knowledge. I stood on the highest hill in Egypt and saw the waters vibrate upon the land. Give me water to drink. Quench my thirst. Give me the power to love.

I've seen the moon fill with rain like a silver cup and I've sailed my boat over heaven. I am the sun roaring beside two lions named Yesterday and Tomorrow. I am a young bull in a field of calves. I have eaten the leg of venison and gnawed the bones of his thigh. I've gone around every island and sailed all the delta canals. I can name every bright lily that grows in Egypt. I am the heir of eternity where the water flows.

20

Water and Fire

I AM THE SERVANT OF RA, eldest son of morning, washing the eyes of gods and bathing in tears. I am the oar of his boat, a strong sycamore hewn for the rowing. I am a friend of water and fire. In this boat I cross the Lake of Flame, ferrying ancient souls. Neither cold nor wet, nor young nor old, we reach the mountain and enter the moment. Against the red sky a young bull stands; sperm falls on the stony plateau. The grapes ripen and grasses grow. He who has no boat disappears in the Lake of Flame. He has no name in the memory of time.

I crossed the river like an old man, ready. I come and go among spotted lions. I have become like the fire and am not burned by fire. Like water I follow myself, flowing on. I am an oar made ready for rowing. Let me lie with the heat of sun in my beard, eating figs and smelling hay. Refresh me with water. Let me enter the temple of fire. Bake me into bread, smelt me into gold.

Fish Stink

IT IS TRUE THAT FISH STINK. It is also true that the river is beautiful. But the river would be beautiful despite the fish. What is noxious remains so.

That is not to say that shit is not useful when buried in the wheat field. Bread made from the field tastes sweet, wine from the arbor sweetest. All things serve a purpose, but that is no reason to glorify what is abominable. A man must still watch where he walks and keep his sandals clean.

22

Not Letting His Heart Be Carried Off

MY HEART. MY MOTHER. MY HEART. My mother. My heart of my becoming. My heart dreams in the house of hearts. My heart sleeps in the house of hearts. My heart ticks in my chest like a beetle. The night waits still; I hear its beating. It resonates like the bow string of an archer. It hums like the string of a lyre. Love. Love. Give me love, sibilant love, thundering love. It is myself that speaks to my heart, my ka, my double. The heart leaps and answers to its name. Its words are the deeds of my body. Its deeds have been my own thoughts, its blood the fluid of gods, river of joy and sadness. My heart leaps like a fish in water. Do not carry off my heart. Do not cut from me my heart.

Beneath the lilies, Ammit stirs—all flesh and teeth and hunger. Orange flames shoot from the corners of her mouth. Beware the eater of hearts. Beware the crocodile, hippo, lion. Beware the snake among the white lilies. When the blue lotus blossoms there my heart stirs within. Turn back, Ammit, you robber of memory. Turn back, oblivion, kidnapper of dreams, pirate of all emotion. Tear not my heart from me. It lives; I live and my fists are strong. Beat. Beat. Beat. No heart shall be given you. No heart shall be eaten. No heart shall beat with my thoughts inside you. No hands shall pluck out my eyes. No twisted fingers shall pierce my red, red heart. No evil words shall ride upon my tongue. My song drifts upward through clouds. In every city above, the gods have dropped to their knees. They put one ear to the ground and listen. Beat. Beat. The music of my becoming.

In my heart are the names of things I have loved—the swallow, the woman, the Nile. In my heart are the deeds my body has done and my heart has been weighed in the balance. I spoke no lies. I squandered no meat. No slander lay on my tongue. To my body I gave the power of my heart. Be, I said, love and create. Beat within. Be gentle. Radiate like sun. And my heart was the launch that ferried me through dark, churning waters. My heart was obedient to the favors of gods. My heart sleeps in the mountain of eternity. Oh, round and pointy-nosed Ammit, pry your fingers from my heart.

My heart is with me, a vessel of dreams, a boat of a thousand men. I am lord of my heart. Beat. Beat. Beat. I am the lion of my heart. I alone have slain its intemperance. I am it—the things I have made. I have lived in truth with my heart. I have lived by the words in my heart. I am a pure man, washed and fasted. I flow in and out of life. My heart pulses with power: water and air. Beat. Beat. Beat. I am an eagle in the light of the sun. The wings beat. I am a lion asleep in the shade. I, myself, am the maker of things that happen. I am the thoughts that passed through me, the love I felt. Let me fly to the far edge of sky. Let me rest in the folds of earth. Let me come at last to the arms of my ancestors. I am a child of eternity.

My heart. My mother. My heart. My mother. My heart is the living heart of earth. My heart is a camel that carries me. My heart is a jug of cool water. My heart is the unblinking eye of night. I spoke no lies. I squandered no meat. No slander lay on my tongue. My heart is a banner unfurled in winds. The goddesses have sent strong breezes. Blessings on thee, my red, red heart. Blessings on thee, my entrails! I dance on the head of a calf under the clouds of heaven and the gods shout blessings. They bang their staves while thunder rolls. I speak their names and grow abundant as reeds. I am earth covered with earth, one with earth, returned to earth. Left in the mountain, I live under the mountain; I am the heart of mountain. I am the rising up, the stirring of bees.

Beat. Beat. Beat. I am life throbbing against the hare's throat. I am a lion with pink tongue lolling. I am my moments in time, the drip of the water clock, the inundation. I am the heart. I rise up. Beat. Beat. I am the fighter, the fire stick raised against darkness, the white knife at the throat of evil. I am the eye plucked by the hand of a demon and who, by the eight gods' grace, had its sight restored. I have spent my hours in battle. I have been bloodied and beaten. I've known the poison and rage that coursed through my body. And I have been a desperate man, a man who lost heart. I have been cowardly and without desire, until at last I called to the gods and they lifted me up. I am recollected and my heart beats again. My heart weeps for my wife and children. My heart weeps for what it remembers. Like a knotting vine, my red blood twists through my body. It binds and strengthens me. I go on. Beat. Beat. Beat.

May my heart increase. May it open wide as sky, enough to hold the breadth of god. May it shape itself into crystal. May a light shine on the hidden things that a man might know himself, his colors, songs and days. May the eight gods whisper secrets. May a man grow great enough to inhabit his own heart. May he walk in it on long roads winding past lotus pools and flowers. May his heart be wide enough to hold the hearts of others. May those he loves link hands, a chain of forever. May his heart and arms and legs be strong and his strength be used for dancing and sowing fields, holding his wife and uplifting their children. May his heart become an altar unto god. May all that passes through be offered to heaven. May the life which touches him, turn again to life. My heart is a field above which the sun rolls. Never-ending beat, beat, beat. May the will of the great heart infuse the body. May the rains come followed by sun, and the green leaves clinging to the vine bend themselves toward light.

23

Not Scattering
His Bones

BIND UP THE BONES IN my back and neck. Wind the sheets tight around me. When the sun returns to these hills and vineyards, I'll rise on my two legs to see. I'll cut my hair, trim and braid my beard, then walk by the Nile where frogs are leaping. I'll dust my feet on the narrow dirt road toward home. I'll pass my house and cats and cattle. Perhaps my wife will wave at my shadow passing. Bind my neck and back for me. Put up the knife, gather my bones and place them in my body. Bind me tight that I may walk. Bind me sturdy that I may stalk after death and strike a blow with the broad, flat sword of my will. I dig my feet into earth. I toss my head to the sky. I am a man living in two worlds. I am a man with two eyes on two legs walking home. Bind my vertebrae with thick grapevines dipped in saffron and water. Cover me with a blanket of sky.

It is as if I had seen my bones for the first time and knew how they fit together, how fitting is the nature of a man to walk. It is as if I fell in love with my bones and was born in their form. I am the banks of the Nile through which living waters flow. My arm calls to my wrist and elbow. My feet speak a language that rattles through my head. The sand beneath dances above in my skull. The honey I've tasted, the lips I've kissed have left their marks upon me. This body is the book of all I remember. These are the bones of a living god. I am the reed from which words flow. Bind up my legs, my back and neck. These bones know where I've been.

24

Not Dying a
Second Time

MY GRAVE IS RIPPED OPEN. My hiding place is revealed. Light tumbles into dark. A carcass, a shell in a sheet. Gold fleck in the eye of a hawk, I spiral away from the grave. I am a child suckling the wolf's teat. The taste of raw milk is sweet. I hide myself in a heart of lapis. Oh, never-setting stars! Oh, trembling brow of Ra! My face is open as a grave. My heart is a casket of jewels. My words are clear-eyed children. I only speak what I know. This story is my bequest.

I am Ra, from whom time began, rising, a red feather in the wind, turning, turning. I am the hub of a wheel, a day star hovering over an endless sea. I am not the harvest; I am the seed. I am not the lyre; I am the song. I will not pass away. I will not pass away.

I will not enter the cavern. The lion's coat turns black in the cavern. I will change myself into a lotus dancing on water. I will not stumble in the cavern. I will follow the sun over the mountain and move on to a land of endless sun. I live for the light. I am that light, a form in the flame when one has gazed long at the fire. I am the oldest child, first-dead son, returning to his mother to suckle. Clouds of heaven tear like a shroud and I see the shine of hidden things. I see myself wrapped in fiery muslin, my face aglow with heat. I see my body crumble away like powder. I smoke like incense. I know the scent of my prayer.

I am the sun on the horizon. I am the song, not the lyre. I will not die a second time. I am coming. I will not pass away. I will not pass away.

25

Not Letting His Head Be Severed

I AM THE SHEPHERD OF birds in branches. I am the son of a shepherd. I am a tongue of fire like the tip of a sword. I am the son of fire. I am the bud of acacia branches. Woe to he who severs his brother's head. Woe to Set who spits in his mother's womb. Do not harm a hair on Osiris' head. Do not touch his burning cheek.

I gather my limbs and bind them in swaddled rags. With the tears of my wife, I make myself whole. I am a green shoot on the olive tree, a chick pipping in the blue egg. I am Osiris, the right eye of my father. I will tie the knots of eternity.

26

Not Decaying in the Other World

BODY, HOW STILL YOU ARE. Are you dreaming? Body, are you thinking of old places, old things? The hands of Osiris lie crossed on his chest, the thumbs touch, two hands like the wings of a falcon. Why do the hands not fly away? Why does the soul not rise up? The fingers of Osiris do not move. They do not take bread to his mouth. His lips are parched. He does not drink wine. His legs will not dance in this darkness. The worm inches through the dust.

Body, rise up singing. May my fingers practice making fists. May my legs quiver and my feet stamp. Body, do not dream the old, easy dreams forever. Flesh, do not rot and stink. Child of sky, child of earth, rise up and speak. Child of dawn, put on your crown. We'll travel far to the desert where the water bubbles up fresh from the rocks, where the olive trees grow low to the ground along the wadi, where the caves are cool and the hermits living there keep their secrets. Rise up, flesh. Do not rot and stink. Do not let my legs be eaten by worms. Do not let darkness overtake me. Body, body, turn to light. Run your fingers through the dust.

27

Not Allowing a Man to Pass East

THEY SAY RA'S COCK IS a golden plow rutting heavenly fields. His seed is the seed that rots in sand and brings up olive trees. Inert for millions of years, I sink into myself and turn to barley. Things happen: light spews over the mountain and I am a wiser man having died in the midst of my living. What I know has been the fruit of years.

Great men follow the path of sun, moment to moment, cycle to cycle. To travel east is to grieve in darkness. They say the night is thick as mucus. The river fills with tears. Blind and dead men pass with shaven heads, lamenting; many men together walk alone in the night. Knife blades ring against the whetstone. In the mountain's belly panthers dream of meat. The flesh of men rots in their teeth. The eyes of dead men are eaten by fish, their noses and fingers and cocks.

I shall not travel east. I shall not fall to forgetfulness, nor lose a moment to desire and regret. Let me gather wheat in its season and swing the scythe. Let me walk under blue skies, weeping. While I live, let my hands build what is mine to build so that I may wake to the sound of cranes. Let me renew myself in light spewing over the mountain, in the voices of gods and the almond trees flowering. I rise upright like the golden cock of Ra, the first-born, the son of my father. Existent for millions of years, I create myself—a man in his moments of time.

Not Losing
His Mind

WHILE I WAS A MAN I walked to the river bank one evening late in summer, and there I waited for the flood. Many months the boats had been tied against the shore. The ropes were tight and the boats banged against dry reeds and rocks. The sailors were long gone home to their wives or to the women in the towns along the river. The night was bright and Sothis, evening's brightest star, had spiraled into being. In the distance I heard women singing and water rushing. A ram came down to the river's edge to drink. I held my wife's hand—we were new lovers then—and I learned the art of inundation.

I am he who stood deep in rising water and dried himself on the bank. I am he who heard beneath the music of hurrying water the laughter of she who in nine months became my daughter. I am he who washed himself in love by the river and became a man on the evening of the New Year. I have been gone these many years and the ram has come again to the bank to drink. I am not there to see it.

Oh, desert wind and swirling sand, mirage of trees in summer! Let me know what is real and not real. Let me see what it is that I have made. Let me see in the mud upon the banks the bricks that will become the houses of cities. Do not let love and happiness make me an idle man. Do not let me become stupid and forget the first time I saw a white ram by the river, drinking. He was the substance of my own thirsty soul. I drank and my mind was made fresh.

I come to this tomb to shed an old skin, to come anew, to rise up like rising water. Do not shut me out from life. Do not let me forget. Do not leave me to stand idle and alone in this hall, surrounded by dreams, for dreams—however beautiful—are vapors and desire, all insubstantial. Give me hands and mind and soul and heart. Give me music, a bright star and some reason to rise and walk. Flood me with purpose and memory. Submerge me in living water.

Coming Forth and Passing Through

THE PLUG HAS BEEN LIFTED from the unguent jar. Oh, cascade of black hair, perfume of the hour. The past has been written, rolled and sealed in a scroll I'll not see again. The eye of the hawk ranges the sky unblinking. Open. Shut. Perfect.

Above olive trees I rise like the sun, like the moon above date palms. Where there is light, I enter absolute. Where there is dark, there is none of me. Like the moon above date palms, I rise. I am counted as one among stars. I am sworn to life. I am bound to death. I take my oath under the sun, splendid eye set ablaze in the forehead of its father.

Oh, beam of light. Oh, sun and moon and stars. Shining beast, man and woman. I pass through. Gaze on me. I've travelled the tomb, dark and lonely. I am now. I have come. I see. This light among the people and along the Nile is my will. In the dark I embraced my father. I burned up night. I killed the snake. I gave him meat. I am his beloved. His time fled through my body—a jolt of essence, a glow of ether, a passion for eternity. I am with him, one of him.

I walk in sleep through heaven. With earth I dust my feet. I have set the sky in two parts. I wander horizons, passing through. In the skins of black panthers, I chant in the ears of children. I am a living god, with the earth millions of years. Coming forth, I pass through.

Bringing Home His Soul

LONELY, I HAVE GONE TO BED, having lit the fire. My soul has been a restless bird that leaves to seek itself. For the hawk who breaks the confines of the shell, even the sky is not enough eternity.

He may be tossed by storms of whirling sand or riding a hot wind above dunes. Far from here his voice may ring through the forests from the branches of a mango. By the Nile he may wait silent among the reeds, catfish spawning as he sleeps, his head tucked in his wing. If you see him, send him home to me. The heart is uncertain country.

I must rise, call the musicians and priests. I must have henna for the heads of dancers. I cannot dream like the idle, sleepless dead. I must rise and stir the fire. Burn moly and saffron; remember my prayers. The smoke of incense will bring him home.

I lie in the valley of a thousand joinings—man to woman, man to dust. Though far and sailing, that ariel of love flies with me. In his copper beak he carries my thoughts. On his back my magnetic and starry dreams fly over mountains, over seas, over villages. Above the grape arbor it is I sailing with the hawk triumphant. Perhaps now he hovers near, flurry of dark wings beating the door; or he follows the rivers and canals of gods, leading them through mountains; or he binds the souls to the rags of mummies, filling dry hands with balsam. Old ones grasp their scepters and rise barefoot in the burning sand. Perhaps he twitters above the barges with their cargos of amethyst, sailing home.

Ah, my soul's a restless bird. Words flow like rivers. Through my veins water churns on; on dark wings he flies from yesterday, love in his throat, the warmth of light among his feathers, the sun risen in his hard, amber eye.

31

His Soul and His Shadow

WHAT CANNOT BE KNOWN REMAINS unknowable, yet I see with the eye of the sun as if it came to rest on my forehead, throwing light in the dark corners of things, casting the shadows of men into uncharted lands. In the houses of the dead the doors are swinging. That which was open has been shut. That which was shut has been opened. Sunlight enters the darkened house and the soul comes home with the umbra.

I have walked that road between mountains, longer than night, whiter than salt, where the hearts of men are made fragrant as hyacinth nodding. To the fields I've travelled and back. I am the same man made new. My hands carry the power of love. I hold my hard, ancient life like crystal. My shadow binds itself to me. My soul whirls, rushing overhead, grazing my hair with the flurry of its wings. Gods sail in the dawn with a cargo of souls waiting to be born. I am the first to walk this road, bringing the reckoning of years. With the eye of sun I see the continuous motion of days, words only silence could have brought to my ears, and light in the eye of the world still to come. My soul, shadow and I are walking.

I know the facts of my life like stones, their various colors and powers. The things I see I've named and remembered. I call to my memories and dreams like children. I've walked the long road and seen the great one napping: old man in the dooryard, the prayers of men like smoke in his beard.

There are those who know nothing of walking in light, who dwell in caves or creep from the rocks, who doubt that the songs of sparrows are real, who live by the club and knife. They would seize a man's dreams and speak them with fetid tongues. They'd tear out his heart and scatter his bones. Their road is dark, but just as well travelled as mine, though their shadows and souls refuse to walk with them.

I see with the sun's eye how doubt under the brilliance of sky causes the clouds to gather. I see I am fire becoming fire, a drop of rain become one with the river. I see the great one weaving a multitude of souls into the threads of his indigo robe. His words are ripe as pomegranates or grapes. His breath is sweet as calamus.

Returning to
See His Home

THE NIGHT SUN RESTS IN the lap of a bear dreaming the northern sky. A half moon, I shine above his legs. I come forth from the edge of heaven. I climb in the deepest pit of sky and rest above cooling rocks, above houses in cities, above people who sleep warm nights on roofs under a half moon dreaming. Oh, I am weak and feeble at the sight of my children sleeping. I am weak with wonder to see my dark wife dreaming. Her hair unbraided and perfumed falls across her eyes, around her firm, brown shoulders, lies wet and dark at the corners of her red, red mouth. I am weak and feeble in cloudless dark, forgetting the teeth and tongues of snakes. I am the night sun in the lap of a bear. I rest above my homeland dreaming.

Below, my house and cattle lie still. I grow stronger, my beams of light like arrows that wound the night, that drive back slick, pale scorpions. I am the eye of a lion who stalks dream fields with his mate. I am a new man full of whistling come home to kiss his wife. High in the dark, a cup of light empties dreams from the sky. A half moon, I sail to the edges of heaven. The wheat in my fields has sprung up in straight rows. I am guardian against forgetfulness, keeping watch, moving on.

Ra Rising

THE NUMBERS OF THE SUN are many; its hours are infinite. Its names are names of things alive. What has form is a part of Ra. With my own eyes I saw him—a brilliant hawk flying into the risings and settings of suns. I tasted god like soup dripping from a ladle. I felt his grace like three lyres humming. Like a single thread that wraps itself around me, he becomes the whole cloth of my being. I am made lively as onions and olives. I walk at peace between lilies and stones.

The strident sun walks through a field of stars. The beautiful one sings in two halves of the sky. Old women sit in their doorways and sniff the breezes. The wind that moves the boats, moves them.

Ten thousand, thousand sticks of light have been raised against the darkness. When the demon falls, his beard is cut. His sinews are torn by the knife.

In this moment the silence of Egypt gathers between the mountains and at the depths of the river. Earth trembles, voiceless as the egg from which the new world rises. Ra is in the wind. He speaks when the earth is silent and he alone existed until he named the name of things. River, he said, and river lived. Mountain. Beetle. Fisherman. From his tongue spring words of water. The river quakes with the sound of his voice. The east wind is the air escaping from his nose. The west wind is a long sigh from his mother. I am fortified by their breathing. My heart bursts into light like a seed. Such things are made every day: duck, mandrake, raisin. Grape, pomegranate and melon. Cypress, palm, Osiris.

34

Awakening Osiris

AIR AND EARTH ARE MY HORIZONS. What lies between is what I am. Oh, infinite form of being! beast and stone and vegetable—the way a man may stand in his garden or dance by the river while wakes of small boats rock the reeds, the cities and the people in them, gods who walk in white linen like women under the blue stone of heaven.

I am the priest in a hidden house, guide to other worlds. I am the idea of myself in my mother's belly, a trembling star in the bright memory of morning, a grain of sand blown east. I am the husband of Isis: woman, widow and witch. On her lips are the charms of ripening wheat; from her arms fly flocks of birds. With a word she drives the snakes from the river and the boats sail far to its mouth.

Air is what I breathe and earth is where I stand. I have given myself to Amentet. It is white with heat. The world is bright as metal. Dead men rise to breathe air and stare into my face, already a yellow disk on the eastern horizon.

A Preponderance of Starry Beings

OH STARRY ONES! I AM a man by a river, gazing up. And how these same stars quiver above Kheraba and An. How these lights reach farther than the watch fires of Heliopolis. And what of hidden things? Oh hawk! oh restless son, sojourner into this season. The snake writhes in your talons. Your wings brush the edge of the sky. Long flight of days passing many lands, death sleeping among many feathers.

Oh soul, ancient ram come here by this pool to drink. Two horns like sense and reason implanted in your forehead. Son of the mountain's sky. Dusty hoof which tramps an old trail. Oh king! This rock on which we live endures. Yours is the white crown and the blue tower of flesh infused with spirit. Above the eye of god dreams us; below we are. Air and earth and mist and fire.

To the east the mountains are singing. Oh lord of acacia trees! whose blossoms are the first sensations, who binds the rags of mummies. This sad mortality! The boat is set upon its sledge and filled with yellow flowers.

Oh jackal Anubis! Show me the road through darkness. I have passed through this door into nothing. Nothing grows and nothing dies; all that was and would be is. This life is a singular breath and your passive eye is time. Oh justice done, truth is law! Upon the brow of men the world is written and in their hearts the word is deed. Smoke from temple fires curl like hair. The ankh in your one hand, the knife in the other.

Oh he whose face is too ponderous for sculpture into stone, Hapi! the waters flow. Papyrus and lotus spring up. In your boat sailing from some unknown city, your body glistens like water.

Osiris. The gods have heard my name. I am a man by the river, gazing up. Husband and tiller and reaper and king, I am lord of seasons, of that which falls and returns to light. I am he who sowed the seed. I am the bread I have made. Eat. This is such nourishing peace.

Adoration of Ra

REJOICING IN THE HOUSES. The sound of brass bells on dancing ankles. The hips of women sway through dusty streets. Day upon day the sun is risen. Day upon day the sun will rise. Day upon day this heat on adobe walls and the splay of light on Osiris. Morning stars and eventide. Chants ring through the valley and across the sands to rise to the altar of heaven. The soul of Osiris walks with wind into the temples of gods. He sets sail in the boat of morning sun. He comes to port at eventide. He twists and twines through star-studded waters, the sound of his oars the ssh-sssh of wind. The sun beats on and on like a tireless heart.

Blessings on thee, hawk, fierce and beautiful as love, whose horizons are the edges of memory so vast a man gets lost. Blessings on thee, beetle sun, which rolls into life every day kicking six legs and humming your shiny ball of song. This world is a little patch of ground you travel with no haste. The sun has burst upon the land, light yellow dust on the head of a bee. The gods are all drunk with light and singing. They crown each other king. The lady of the great house weaves garlands on his forehead. Vines and flowers of the twelve cities meet themselves. "My lord," she says, "the sun is bright today. It hovers between your shoulders." The idea of himself travels with him, affixed like the figurehead of a ship. His enemies beat themselves with sticks, tumble and sink beneath black waters. From the netherworld the dead arise to glimpse his shining face. The sea is pregnant with form. And the belly of sky is beautiful.

Every day, the sun. Every day. And I walk east in the garden to see you, west through the country to be with you. Oh sun, my head fills with light. Do not turn me from your easy lust, whole in the sky, white with heat. Do not bind me in sheets of darkness, a worm in the brown cake of earth. My hands are bread I have made every day. The sun spins into my heart, a place where sparrows nest. I am ridiculous and rolling on the ground, pleased with such company. Every day, the sun on the wall, light lingering on a ripe fig. I am he who worships the sun, a space in my heart a bird could fill. I am one who listens to the grass speaking in the garden. May I chew the green blade of eternity in a garden filled with sun. May I walk into fire and be burned like kernels of wheat, ground into the pulp of existence. May the sun pound and bake me brown as bread. May I rise like bread every day.

In the field with my cattle, my shadow sinks into black earth and rises. The smell of things growing. The sky and horizon part like waking lovers; like a child, the sun rises from their sleep. The world watches its steps—old man, old child, old king, sun passing in the sky, light of all that can be said, shadow of hidden things. Every face watches, every eye turns; resplendent dawn and evening. Such passion is existence. Every day my liege rides his boat, glory dripping like water from an oar. Every day the streets churn with people, every face turning. Such power cannot be measured. Such love cannot be told. Unspeakable grace in the fields and cities. I dip my bread in milk and eat.

Mantis, this landscape is hidden from all but the most holy eye. Oh sun going out to the sea's edge over the crest of mountain, what might a weary man call home but the light in his head, the scroll in his heart? What darklings wait with blood red teeth within the walls of his sacred home? Such country the sun has seen, truth like memory or love. Such colors of robes some women wear, more mauve than grapes their gowns and eyes. What is hidden belongs to the sun. It is too much for a man to know. It is Ra who gathers the world together, who holds and beholds with his eye, this juxtaposition of vegetation and air, the thousand colors of prayer and stone. Having sprung from formless water, he takes his shape in fire. He springs from the mouth of the horizon as if he were the first word he uttered. May he string his words into song. May he roll through the heavens like music. And for as long as the sun is singing, may the strings of my soul hum like a lyre.

Sun, your number is one multiplied by millions. I am but a man with my thousand longings for unity. May we never cease to be. May there be no time in which a man must count the days toward some end. Oh, that life could be more than its fragments. No before and no after, no exaltation but in the timeless one. The sun strides over heaven crossing distances of millions of years and the hundreds of thousands of millions ... one day of the sun. He set-rises, set-rises over thousands of cities, trees and mountains and men. The distance of the instant. He has made an end to hours and likewise counted them. In the morning earth fills with light. Law and baptism. The one of us all endures. It is our work under the sun.

Speak of the rising heart of carnelian. Red heart of a living god, old priest in an ancient tomb, an image scratched into muscle and blood. On this stony plateau we stand, all our days like beads of lapis strung on the throat of sky. We stand—existent cities washed with color, ash of night fallen underground. The great world pours out its unguents and the little world is made great. A shout among many people rises on a day of splendor when the sun folds back on itself. He deepens and lengthens and thickens, molding his body with light. The sun grinds itself like corn. Tendrils of fire seek their limits of light. This is the color of time, the joy and pain of a birthing mother. He is born in the form of Ra. He creates himself on his mother's thigh.

May I reach an everlasting heaven and walk in the legend of mountains with thoughts quiet as deer. May I meet myself in every vegetable and rock quickened by tendrils of light. Holy and perfect is the world which lives by fire in the embrace of the carnelian heart. May I walk with the sun until eventide, forgetting the reason of hours. May I burst into light like a purple flower remembered by a lover.

The sun has risen like gold or wheat, aurora in the land of his birth, splendor in a country of sky. His mother is draped in a gauze of air, the disc revolves in her hand like a bowl of meal. Egypt will be fed. Great light bursts on the horizon and men who've slept in the dark with stomachs empty as night rush into the streets hungry, happy to eat morning. Ten thousand thousand fingers wash in the flood, ten thousand thousand grapes and olives feed on living water. In the towns and in the temples there is a festival, flood of wine and flowers, one song many lutes are playing. A woman suckles her baby, while her husband drunk with meat and beer lies in the shade of a fig tree, singing praises to her inner thigh.

Might of might. Splendor of splendor. This is the terror inherent in love: that such power may exist without reason, that death may be feared and lusted for as a woman, that passion gives rise to passion. I am moved by desire as if a boat transported me from horizon to horizon. What I have done for love, let it be held against me. I am a man whose heart is full. I am a man empty of sin. It is life I desire. My lust for it and I enter the heart of the mountain together. Together we are judged by shining beasts and they say, "There walks he who loves his life."

One day with a shout I'll rise through the sky. My voice will mingle with air. I'll cross horizons. With silver wings I'll enter the realm of magic. Within the temple of mountain and sky, corn grows amid earth's yellow scars. This is the sacred cathedral of Ra into which men long to enter. My name recalls the countless stars under which new lovers kiss. Death ferries me to a distant shore while striped fish spawn on turquoise waters, while black fish leap in white rivers.

The universe is drawn in circles. The memory of chariot wheels clacking across small stones foreshadows the asp's death as he wraps himself around the wheel. He is crushed by its embrace. The air crackles when Ra is within. And sailors, who've known only cities by the sea and the whip of the rope and sail, come to moor at last amid a crush of flowers and rejoice and weep and go on. The days before and the days after fill with the odor of pomegranates. The heart ripens like fruit, falls and breaks. Sweet meat for the lips of gods. On such a day one glances into the sky and finds the eye of Ra looks back. One finds loaves of bread on fine reed mats and the eye of Ra looks back. The air crackles. The sun beats on and on.

A Messenger of Ra

THIS BOAT WAS HEWN OF cypress wood seven arms in length, green as crystal tourmaline, strong as the voice of Ra. The world has spread itself before me, washed with natron and ambergris. I sail through stars silver as fishes. I am a messenger of Ra. What grace I've seen no man can know: green words fly from the mouths of gods; ground and baked, red words rise like bread—a perfect food for dead men. Yellow stone in the sea, golden light among stars, I am a messenger of Ra whispering the secret of ages.

In the Talons of the Hawk

THE SNAKE WILL RISE TO heaven in the talons of the hawk. In their season a thousand boats sail. Forever shadows and light clutch the world and the river floods. Men rise to walk, full of themselves, inundating earth with life. Such is the way of existence—the empty filling and the full emptying. In their season date palms grow. The earth covers you and in your season you rise. From the blue egg was born dark and light.

When you see the slaughterer, kiss him and fall down. His sword is swift. It brings you life. You shall die and rise as Osiris, born in the magic of sky. Suckled by the mother's teat, you will learn the nature of love. In your hands the slaughterer places the sword with which you must conquer darkness. You shall live not by faith, but with certainty; not in sacrifice, but in ecstasy, and know the coming and going of flowers, the passion of love, of loss and pain.

In my hand I took the sword I was given and I learned to use it. I severed the heads of the children of darkness and felt no pity for the fallen. I brought suffering and pain, but wicked men grieved and were changed. Blood ran through the fields. Wheat grew waist-high. Green was the color of grace.

Those who saw light and remained unchanged fell to the earth and became asses, into the water and became fish. Their names shine in heaven no longer. Though they see Egypt's people pass through the house of heaven and walk earth's fields again, though they watch boats sail on waters and lotuses float beneath stars, though they pray, their prayers are unanswered. Neither born again nor dying, they remain in silence, unchanged; without soul or form, less than the air between us they are. Nothing.

Therefore, when I saw darkness in myself, I cut it from me and wept for the pain was unbearable. Blind and mourning, I stumbled into the desert, scooping up the blue virtue of sky and setting it in my heart. Then my heart flew out and circled above like a hawk. It joined a thousand birds circling, serpents writhing in their talons. And I wept, for without love or loss or pain I would not have known this happiness.

There is joy on earth and in heaven—joy unimaginable. In every blade of grass rises the strength of the sun. In every mortal shines the star of immortality. All things demand adoration and respect. In each child an old man lies coughing and dying, and in old men fresh children are singing. Though dead perhaps a million years, each day I sail with the sun. On my lips the taste of frankincense hangs. The soles of my feet are perfumed with myrrh. Above the fields of malachite golden hawks fly and, in gold upon golden tablets, the gods write. Let men sing loudly and cast incense in the fire. Let ducks be roasted. In this world the sun rises. The sky is unbound. Rains fall to take our thirst. We breathe beneath heaven and upon the earth, in the presence of gods and goddesses.

And the quiet that settles on our skin before dawn keeps company with those whose dreams are troubled.

Before Changing

ONCE THE WORLD WAS FORMLESS and empty with night until found by the light and filled. Under a moon both dark and bright, man grew half-obscured, while olive branches bent toward the light and roots dug deep in clay darkness. We create ourselves in the forms we imagine. Years pass. We are what we have spoken.

Where there is a road an old man walks thinking, bent under the weight of his soul clinging like a child to his back. Ra spits his words into the dirt where they cover themselves and wait like seeds. The wheat will rise up singing. The old man walks in circles beneath the circling sun. He makes a journey for himself from mewling infant to old man, old man to renewed god.

The snake comes to take his heart, finding there the sun.

Where there is sky Ra goes sailing and dead men rise to meet him, casting no shadow on the roads, but for their souls like thick clouds passing. All the gods are following as the Great One rolls around, one with the wind, swallowing breezes. Somewhere on a patch of ground a tired ox slavers in the wind, heat dripping from his tongue. The air is cool in the season of planting and a man may be at home in his body. In his house he eats and praises the meat between his teeth. The earth and men are a kind of truth.

A beam of brightest sun falls like a word against the grave. A new man has taken his boat for an afternoon of fishing. The dead dream quietly, counting their bones, turning in their rags toward the city of death—Amentet, the beautiful. They will walk again.

40

Becoming the Swallow

IN THE DARK MARROW OF my bones I have made myself light. I am the swallow spinning at dawn, through whom light enters sky, who flies formless above a world of forms, ringing across the horizon. We make of ourselves what we imagine. I command scorpions to lie still. I open the east doors of heaven; arrows fly quick as light. I am a swallow like no other, full of magic, a daughter of Ra. Among gods and goddesses I live on air perfumed by clove and temple fires. I am a crystal where dark shapes enter and fill with color. Sunlight filters through each feather. In the light I quiver and whirl, and I know what shadows my passing throws to the ground.

It is morning in the noisy cities, on mountains where earth enters sky, in the cupped hands of beggars yawning on every street corner, and in the small dark mouth of a bird. Stretch out your hands filled with red barley, and I shall eat. Let me speak of all I have seen.

All days are but one day lived on the Island of Flame. Ra rises up as a column of fire and from him issue children bright and smoldering as metal, countless lights swirling in liquid darkness. His head throbs, then cracks like a blue speckled egg and the flaming sun rolls out. His words like swallows fill the air, and like a fine dust morning settles on the eyelids of sleepers.

Now is the day of reckoning when years laid end to end are numbered, when travelers huddled about the night fire hear the story of every man. The doors of the past and future open. I must speak of it. I was like Horus, prince of the air, son of Osiris, grandchild of Ra, blind in one eye until the moon rose. I sail at dawn and pass between two worlds. To the sky I am a thing of bone and earth; to the earth, I am partly sky. My face is the mirror, within my eye spins living fire. Dawn and dusk, I am the swallow skimming—vagabond, servant and god.

Though born of air, he who has not the imagination to fly falls to earth and grovels with worms. But he who believes is lifted by belief and returns to air, to the cool sweet milk of his mother.

I have lain at the feet of the world and felt its power pass through me. Dead I stood naked before the judged and I was pierced by truth. Down I fell and labored like a woman. I wept, I laughed, I was ashamed. I sang and in time I was made new. I bring the story of light: how I climbed the ladder of heaven, how with my wings I brushed the edges of stars and flew straight to the heart of the universe. Look at me, at my eyes. All I've seen is captured there. Look on the world built by magic and know the hearts of its children.

I have held my destiny in my two hands and I am the shape I made. I have suffered and loved. I have walked through fire and did not burn. I've been blown by wind and did not fall. I've walked the long road and kept to my journey though I met no other traveler. I have lost and found myself in every rock, field and tree. I know what I am and what I imagine. I know shadow and light, and I have never been satisfied with shelter and bread when the great was left unattained.

This I have done to enter death and turn from nothing toward life. I shall pass into heaven, even I shall pass like eternity, quietly in the fire and flesh.

41

Becoming the Falcon of Gold

I RISE ABOVE THE CRESCENT moon to the seven stars, beyond the history of men, beyond numbers and words that bind us. From the earth I rise like a falcon of gold released from a blue egg. I fly above and below the great worlds. I take the shape of a young boy working. In my belly I carry the seed that becomes me. Praise the corn that rots and the sedge that rises. Praise the emerald heart of earth. Praise the coming and going of creatures, the constancy of the world and the word.

I come from light and to light I return. My talons grasp the ring of colors: the gold beak of dawn, the blue eyes of day, the deep red blood of dusk. I rise. In truth I burst on the world like an arrow flung from darkness, sparks of fire from my forehead like burning stars streak the sky. I gather myself, thought and bone, and burst again into flight. I soar and know the god who speaks with the voice of flame.

I am one of the great ones sitting in a field of corn. I eat and I am nourished. In turn I offer myself, the bread of air, the white spirit of fire. I am a falcon of gold. I burn with a passion and lie still. I flare and smolder, live and die in a breath. I sail on gold wings that fan the blaze. I am consumed by fire. This is what I was born to: to live, to love, to know, to change and embrace the infinite. I shall not forget my becoming.

42

Becoming the Hawk Divine

IMAGINE THE ANCIENT ONE SPEAKING as if you were his dream—old lips grown yellow and hard, dry as bone, his mouth a beak that crushes words like seed and after a long flight drops them to grow again in a field left untended. Imagine his eyes, amber orbs that search and catch upon the shallow breaths of a mouse stirred by restless dreams of corn. Hollow bones become swift wings and in his dark, finely feathered skin you ride through all the lost days. Above blinding white cliffs you soar and find yourself amid rocks crumpled like paper, rocks sharp as knives, rocks heart-breakingly real as breasts. Blessed are the old ones. They shall die and soar above themselves, new men again, swift birds, strong oxen, gentle flowers nodding.

The ways have been arranged that I might know my own passage. I have loved the light and followed it easily and with joy. And I struggled to learn how to lie with the darkness where all the wrong things happened for the right reasons.

The ways have been arranged. I circle the heads of dancing girls, my feathers tremble in their fans; I fly above the smoking kilns where brown bread was baked and clay vessels were made strong or shattered. I circle the houses where I laughed and wept, dreamed and made healthy children. Through me the past flows like blood. Vultures gobble the sin with the flesh. Let the devils who beat an old man with their fists lie in a grave of worms. Let bad debts be repaid by the blow of sticks. Let the sun that rode on my back light my face. Let the earth be pounded by dancing feet on slender ankles. Let the young, white ram come to the river to drink and admire his new horns in the water. Let night fall with all the finality of death and I shall see a single star. Though the crescent moon pass through me like a slender knife, though it touch me, I shall live.

Then as men celebrate the coming light, I shall pass into darkness. I shall wander the night stumbling and falling. I shall embrace the great nothing—a shadow so deep it encompasses all, unseen but felt in the hearts of men as the sorrow, the loss, the death. And I shall bless the void for it prepares me, leaves me empty so that light may enter.

In my weakness the dark shall cover me with the red cloth of death and the hungry leopard shall pass by as if I were less than shadow. I shall hide even as the gods hide behind the veil of nothingness, listening. Though they hear men call in their troubles, they come not; yet silent, beyond the veil their shining fingers move, weaving the cloth of destinies. Even great gods are bound by law not to interfere with a man's own becoming. Therefore, we die and lie alone awaiting transformation.

The gods care not if you rage and thrash your breast. They hear not words but thoughts. They speak not to ears. Be silent then and let them speak to the god within. Be quieter still and let the will speak through you.

Oh ancient one who names and dreams the ways, give me air alive. Grant me the revolution, the change, the great doubling-back-on-itself. Let our hearts' truth entwine like terror and tenderness. Awaken me with tender dreams as if with your mouth against my ear, your hot words entered me. Let me know the great change and the small ones that I may see your hand on all things—the frog, the lotus and me. May all the world envelop me that I might know the conversation of wind or the willful flight of a bee, that I might become the song of earth and turn again to greening. Let me walk through the fields sure of the ways that brush my thighs gentle as flowers.

Let one song rise from the universe. Let the souls of all things tremble as the wind stirs blades of grass. I will sit in the midst of its blue wonder as if that song were struck on my bone and sinew. Let the ground beneath me shake. Let the gates of heaven open pouring down silvered hours. Let me walk under the spell of a dark moon in the light of my own divinity. May I live in clouds and growing corn and in the rock bed or the rising river. May I fall like rain and rise like sedge. May I soar the empty place of sky like a hawk whose wing tips brush the gold and crimson reaches of dawn. May I gaze on the knot of eternity wherein the threads of our fates are tied—man to woman, fire to water, earth to sky. May I lie down with magic and hear the secrets of days and weeks in her kiss. May I spend long years talking with the fig trees. May I speak with he who speaks our destinies. May I walk in thunder and rain with the god of change. May I travel the bright paths even into darkness, for I am a sharp and shining thing. By the light within me I shall see the burdens and joys of love. I shall be like the shining falcon wandering in and out of heaven, like the white ibis in the river gazing on fishes.

I change as the old ones before me changed, constantly and with rejoicing. I live not in the memory of my bones, but in the fresh grass of the fields. I am not what I was nor yet all I will be. I am an old man grown young. To me was given the truth of the ways, the swallows and the fishes. If I please I walk among the living cities, going along the warm and dusty paths I've known, unseen as the air that rocks between two sisters, visible as light. I am as worthy of love as truth—that I exist is truth itself. My body is but wax and wick for flame. When the candle burns out, the light shines on elsewhere. What matters is the word whispered at birth, the spark flown from infinite fire. I breathe inside the bright word, the truth, the circle. I burn like a secret in the heart of the mountain. I am an idea wrapped in flesh that sprang from the belly of sky. I am light from the bright vortex of fire from which even first light came, and that which made the maker of gods and men, lights the black world in the blink of an eye. In my joyous and eternal changings, I come to know that that eternally unchanges, for in my becoming I change into everything and what changes not is all already. That fire has made me glorious and given me glad weeping; I, who sprang from the lashes of its eye, am longing to go home, to rest in the fire that gave me birth, to count myself among the absolute that dwells in the numberless one.

I know the language of birds, the augury of dawn and the light of days. I know the melody of splendor before the dream of time began. Before my birth huge gods and strange beasts whispered. It was said I should fly from the eye of sun, even that I should die and my belly swarm with worms, that I should soar like a hawk, the snake writhing in my claws. All I am and shall be were fixed at birth by the cry of birds. And I shall live forever.

And I shall live forever.

Before the hawk sailed beneath the moon, before magic made the word, before Isis birthed her orphaned son, I flourished in the mirrored sea. I grew strong, then waxed old, bent as the crescent moon, an ancient man full of wise dreaming. I ruled the night with its thousand lights and brought the stars to rest behind the shadow of hills. As time passed and I grew from lightness to dark, I learned the power of hidden things. Like a hawk I sailed beyond the known into the realm of what must be imagined. I learned the power and shape of sleep and molded silence into dream. These dreams I filled with hearts and minds that they might love, and they became men, myself. Who knows how long these changes took—an hour, or a thousand years. I was long in my dreaming beneath the earth. Time had no reach. Two lions lay at my feet devouring the children of the past and future. When the dream was done, like a hawk I rose and two clouds closed behind me, then it was as if I'd never left the sky. Birds sang. Lilies opened their spathes. On the air I heard the word and felt the wheel of change. I learned to read the movement of clouds and walk the roads in blessed forgetfulness that all roads might seem travelled fresh.

I, who took possession of hidden things, learned the language of hawks. I was given the eyes and heart of the bird, the power of the cry and claw. In the years that passed, in the wind about my head, I heard the voices of the old ones. "The past and future dream us, lie on our bodies like skin that we might pass the days with grace. To us were given all the ways and the obligation to travel. To us were opened all the roads of heaven, all the tunnels in earth and the channels of the sea. Among the dead and the living, by these same words have we all travelled. Together we walk a single path into the heart of the infinite."

Now the treasures of the world lie before me—the jeweled wings of love and the gold bracelets of days. The crown of existence rests on my head, crystal stars in a lapis sky. Tempted neither by terror nor wonder, I take earth's simple offerings: a handful of seeds, the air in my nose and the rays of light on my belly. In time I'll fly in and out of time. In time I'll come to the house of magic. I shall pass into the unity of fire and know dreams and colors and secrets. For now it is enough to roam the air that separates earth from sky. I do not hurry my destiny. I neither long for history nor forget it.

I am the hawk, glorious hawk, soaring hawk beneath the sun. Bands of light wreathe my head. I own the property of day. On swift wings I've flown to the edges of the world, cutting a path to the far reaches of heaven. Back I fly and hover over splendid fields. I've grown old and wise as a god. The sky wraps her arms about me; the earth kisses my feet. The goddesses tear their veils for me and I walk into the eye of fire. Ah, the things I see when the flame bursts forth. I look on the dust of life with eyes of fire. I rise from dust and spin. Life opens its mouth and swallows me. And I live to walk familiar streets, see old friends, tell their children stories. I speak of the journey through blood into paradise—how the gods of the other world tried to turn me from the path that held my destiny, how I travelled through night in a dim confusion of stars, how desert beasts tore my heart with their claws, how I lived and my spirit grew until I felt no pain even in the teeth of the great devourer, how I stood inside the heart of fire, burning and was made new. I am that bright fire. It lives in me. Lift your faces that you might see.

I was given the heart of the sky, the soul of a hawk, the wisdom of stars. I become what I must to understand each season that passes in the heart of a man—jealousy, rage, bitterness, hope, trust, ease . . . And I know that change is a difficult task, a dying, a dreaming, an awakening.

Alone I make my way along the bright paths of the valleys, through the cooling shadows to the mountain of regret. In dark caves I hear the howling of dogs or children, while far off the yellow sands blow and young bulls clash horns in distant fields. I listen to the sounds of life's reckoning. "Silence," I cry and the night is still. It's so quiet I can hear the long grasses the cattle have eaten turning into dreams. Then before dawn, before the last star fades and the first swallow cries, I feel light enter my fingers. How even everything that has changed, changes.

What a long road it seems I've travelled. The beauty and terror of it! The crying of the gods or children, the yellow flowers calm in the last gold light. The names of all the powers seem shouted out by blades of grass, by clouds, by rocks underwater, by the darkness in the mouths of caves, by dead men under the burning sand and in the hearts of mountains. Let me hurry to them then as a man hurries home to rest after a long day in the fields. I've gathered and tied my life to my waist like the pelts of magical animals. Nothing common or rare escapes me. I carry the power within. I've fallen face down upon the earth to gain the power of heaven, powers greater than the ceaseless shining of stars, powers as great as the sun at creation. Having lived the life demanded of me, I shall step into eternity. Long and quietly I spoke with my soul of death, of love, of things that mattered. I am clothed in light, loved and touched by light, bound by light to enter light. On my heart I bear the scars to prove I lived and I live still. And I live forever. I've been shamed and beaten and have cried out for revenge as I gazed on the empty face of sky. I learned the story of my existence as I lived it, as it was spoken from the mouths of gods. I've passed through the terrors of night. Thirsty and tired I fell by the roadside. I've lifted my face to eternity and been blessed by the kiss of morning.

Now, like a hawk I rise into air, into the heart of the universe. I rest on clouds, hearing joyful things—the song of sparrows, the buzzing of bees, the laughters and pleas of courtesans, the wind murmuring in carob trees. I am whirring as a hawk. With the eyes of the hawk I see, think his thoughts and know the joy of his heart. My flesh is vibrant as air, my words sharp and long as a shout.

Today all the old men in heaven are happy. They are made strong as bulls in green pastures, ready to run, to snort and bellow, ready to make many children. Today is the last day of the world. The sun will not set, the light never wane. We've reached the knot of eternity. A million million years are with us. The breath of life enters. Rivers flow unending. Great is the power of the human heart to love, to change, to make new. The word of light has been spoken and has lived by our hands, in our bodies and in the things we made. Truth shall not pass away. As I turn to dust, I turn to light. I have come home to my father, my brothers, my children, my friends. I have come home to myself. Though my house falls to dust and my fields turn to sand, the light of Egypt lives a million years in me. I shall enter the eye of fire forever. I shall gaze into fire and find the comfort of wife, children, home and cattle. In the dream of an old man, in the eye of eternity, I shall live forever.

43

Becoming One of the Ancients

LIKE A FISH IN WATER, like a lapwing among stars I breathe among the gods. I have lived among gods countless years. I am an old soul, a great man, one of the ancients. Many nights I have looked into the fire, felt the heat of their tongues, seen their faces, heard them speaking. Many days I have stopped behind my plow to gaze up, blind with the sun and the gods' power. In my times, and there have been many times, I have come to know the gods. By their silence I understand their presence. I have quivered beneath the power of their hands on my head and trembled in the powerlessness of their absence when they turned and left me to my destiny.

At dawn beyond the ring of trees, the great one comes like the golden eye of a hawk opening, like the wind that moves the boats, his breath caught in a tattered white sail. With invisible hands he tugs on the green shoots causing corn and wheat to rise. The first among us, he willed himself to be, then in his loneliness dreamed the company of others. Because he willed it ripples formed on the water and clouds billowed in the sky. Because he willed it stars spewed from his lips and the sun and moon sprang from his eyes. Because he willed it he gave power to lesser gods the way a mother gives bread to her children. They, in turn to please him, made fish in the sea, birds in the air and wheat in the fields. Because he willed it men and women leapt forth and made children, tamed cattle, harvested barley. Because it pleased him he made these things and lay destiny upon them. What passes, what is and what will be are the stuff of the old man's dreams. One day he'll wake and all he has made to flourish will wither. He will coil round himself, a snake devouring his children, then slither away with us all in his belly. And we shall go away with him knowing what a good dream it was.

He sleeps. A new dream begins.

I am an old man, an ancient one, and I have been many things, lived and died many times, and loved as often as possible. And I tell you the gods exist within the limits of every thing—stone or vegetable, woman or man. Even the red clay the potter molds hides their essence. That a creature or thing exists makes it one with god. Blessed are we all. Because we exist we live for eternity as women or men, birds or fish, stones or wheat, dust in the wind. We shall be what we imagine though we know not yet what that may be. Blessed are we in eternal changing. We live among gods because we are gods. Blessed are the creatures and gods of earth, things of the air and water, flame from the fire.

I have lived in the midst of gods who knew not who they were. You and I are pure as dream, lasting as words, opulent as women. We were given the gift of becoming and the ways of it. After a time of forgetting, I come back to myself. I am as tied to my destiny as an ass is tied to its plow. Because the gods will it, the work is done, and our labor to become what we must is like the perfume of lotus and red sanders.

I have taken pains to empty myself of the illusions of flesh, to accept failure, even success when it comes, but not to crave it as some men crave wine. I have looked into my heart and seen jealousy, pride and greed. I've seen fear and resistance to change. Even as I cast these off as a snake sheds skins, I've been tempted to congratulate myself. I have regretted the past and longed for the future, forgetting to notice the mountain of the present. But today, for this moment, I am here with you unburdened by thought and filled with joy. In this moment I regret nothing for the paths I chose led me here. I offer you my life. In this moment as the veil opens and before it closes, I see us as we are—that we are gods, that all that exists and can be named is god coming from the body of god. If I but touch the present, I shall know what lies before and behind for these, too, are holy members of his body. I am, therefore, a god among you, born in the company of men. I tell you in truth, here, in my field behind this sometimes slow and stubborn donkey, I am standing before god. It is good to be here.

Becoming the Craftsman

I EAT THE BREAD I BAKED. I drink the beer I brewed. I drape myself in white linen woven by my own hands. Making. Making. Making. My spirit lifts on the wings of a golden hawk. I am the cackle of joy in the throat of the wild goose. I am a child in awe of my own power, filled with wonder, bewildered, awake. I am one of the wonders of earth, full of blood and breath and singing. Even as I dance toward the mountain, even as I dance toward death, I celebrate my marvelous being. I dance with the great ones who writhe and chant, who conjure spirit, the light in the darkness.

Truth lies on the hearts and tongues of men. Speak and live. You are creator and creation. Your life is craft, your supple body molded by word, sculpted by desire, fired by deed. You poise yourself between life and fate, the will of men and the will of gods. In the beat of a heart, the suck of breath, you are the universe. Making. Making. Making.

I have heard lies, yet have not believed them. No matter the pain, I shattered illusions. I sought the crack in every cup. The things said of me in anger or in praise I have not made my own. It is for my conscience to guide my hand, my deed to create myself. I am myself perceiving myself, making, making, making.

In those moments of silence when desire and will are stilled, I know the purpose gods know. My body is nourished by the things of earth, my spirit by the things of the heart. Under flowering almond trees I eat the fruit of love. I watch boughs dance in the wind, hear wavering music in dreams. I am making, making, making. I offer what I have made—my bread, my peace, myself. I wrap my skin in the blue robe of heaven. I sit in the garden listening to birds. I do what my heart tells me. My thoughts leap visible as light. I am what I know, what I feel, what I make. I am myself, the ether of the instant, breathing. I gather and build my life. The earth is a small globe created by thoughts, mine and those of others. I walk among houses, the fields, flowers and rocks, even the poison of snakes, the sting of bees are mine. All existence is the measure between light and dark, bees and serpents, wind and fire. I love the scorpion, yet I know its poisonous sting. To live in harmony is a beginning.

What can be named can be known, what cannot be named must be lived, believed. I speak of the creator and the creation, the ordinary life lived extraordinarily. I work for the sake of working. The joy of creating is the joy of forgetting everything else. I lean into life. My tongue is fire; my breath is wind. The spirit spits from my mouth. I speak of a chain of events where making leads to making, action to action, love to love, where the beginning began so long ago we find ourselves always in the midst of it.

There is no rest. The act is now. In your lives you will make children, make peace, make errors, you will make trouble, you will dance under the sun and moon. As long as you live you will create life. You will rise and fall many times. It is like the making of a good loaf of bread. You will be nourished.

Becoming the Child

IN SEAFOAM, IN SWIRLINGS AND imaginings I am fish, tadpole, crocodile. I am an urge, an idea, a portent of impossible dreams. I lie between heaven and earth, between goodness and evil, patience and explosion. I am innocent and rosy as dawn. I sleep with my finger in my mouth, the cord of life curled beside my ear. Like a child in its mother's belly, I am with you but not among you. I know no ending for I have no beginning. I have always been here, a child in the silence of things, ready to wake at any moment.

I am possibility.

What I hate is ignorance, smallness of imagination, the eye that sees no farther than its own lashes. All things are possible. When we speak in anger, anger will be our truth. When we speak in love and live by love, truth in love will be our comfort. Who you are is limited only by who you think you are. I am the word before its utterance. I am thought and desire. I am a child in the throat of god. Things are possible—joy and sorrow, men and women, children. Someday I'll imagine myself a different man, build bone and make flesh around him. I am with you but a moment for an eternity. I am the name of everything.

I've dreamed the nightmare a hundred times, that old revulsion of bone and flesh, waking in sweat, in a headlong rush toward the world, into the cool certainty of fires that burn in sudden stars, the heat in the body. That I am precludes my never having been.

What I know was given to me to say. There is more.

There are words that exist only in the mind of heaven, a bright knowing, a clear moment of being. When you know it, you know yourself well enough. You will not speak. I am a child resting in love, in the pleasure of clouds. I read the book of the river. I hold the magic of stones and trees. I find god in my fingers and in the wings of birds. I am my delight, creator of my destiny. It is not vanity.

There are those who live in the boundaries of guilt and fear, the limits of imagination. They believe limitation is the world. You cannot change them. There is work of your own to do. You will never reach the end of your own becoming, the madness of creation, the joy of existence.

Dance in the moment. Reach down and pull up song. Spin and chant and forget the sorrow that we are flesh on bone. I return to the rhythm of water, to the dark song I was in my mother's belly. We were gods then and we knew it. We are gods now dancing in whirling darkness, spitting flame like stars in the night.

In the womb before the world began, I was a child among other gods and children who were, or may be, or might have been. There in the dark when we could not see each other's faces, we agreed with one mind to be born, to separate, to forget the pact we made that we might learn the secrets of our fraternity. We agreed to know sorrow in exchange for joy, to know death in exchange for life. We were dark seeds of possibility whispering. Then one by one we entered alone. We walked on our legs, and as we had said, we passed in well-lit streets without recognizing each other; yet we were gods sheathed in flesh, the multitude of a single spirit. Gods live even in darkness, in the world above your heads, in the crevices of rocks, in the open palms of strangers.

I am a child, the seed in everything, the rhythm of flowers, the old story that lingers. Among cattle and fruit sellers, I am air. I am love hidden in a shy maiden's gown. I am the name of things. I am the dream changing before your eyes. I am my body, a house for blood and breath. I am a man on earth and a god in heaven. While I travel the deserts in frail form, while I grow old and weep and die, I live always as a child inside the body of truth, a blue egg that rocks in the storm but never breaks. I sleep in peace in my mother's lap, a child mesmerized by sunlight on the river. My soul is swallowed up by god.

Out of chaos came the light.

Out of the will came life.

Becoming the Lotus

AS IF I'D SLEPT A thousand years underwater I wake into a new season. I am the blue lotus rising. I am the cup of dreams and memory opening—I, the thousandpetaled flower. At dawn the sun rises naked and new as a babe; I open myself and am entered by light. This is the joy, the slow awakening into fire as one by one the petals open, as the fingers that held tight the secret unfurl. I let go of the past and release the fragrance of flowers.

I open and light descends, fills me and passes through, each thin blue petal reflected perfectly in clear water. I am that lotus filled with light reflected in the world. I float content within myself, one flower with a thousand petals, one life lived a thousand years without haste, one universe sparking a thousand stars, one god alive in a thousand people.

If you stood on a summer's morning on the bank under a brilliant sky, you would see the thousand petals and say that together they make the lotus. But if you lived in its heart, invisible from without, you might see how the ecstasy at its fragrant core gives rise to its thousand petals. What is beautiful is always that which is itself in essence, a certainty of being. I marvel at myself and the things of earth.

I float among the days in peace, content. Not part of the world, the world is all the parts of me. I open toward light and lift myself to the gods on the perfume of prayer. I ask for nothing beyond myself. I own everything I need. I am content in the company of god, a prayer that contains its own answer. I am the lotus. As if from a dream, I wake up laughing.

Becoming the Snake

THE STORY GOES THAT CHANGE is inevitable. So it must be that having eaten dust and rotting flesh, the snake comes to know in his own skin the secrets of change.

Through the deceit of death I grow wise in the illusions of time. I change, I grow beyond myself, leaving the papery sheath that once was what I was. I live alone and make my changes in secret. I know the smell of fear, of death, of innocence. I float among lilies. I rest in shadows. I lick the wisdom of air and dust. I know the earth, sky and men. I wrap myself around the legs of life. By the enmity of others I learn empathy with all creatures. I lie down in darkness and learn the art of subtlety. I rear and strike in surprise. I know the limits of earth. In my belly I know this is all one place. I leave but a meandering trail in the dust, a graceful passage like the tracings of time. I lie down and change and rise and grow old and lie down and change and rise. I demand neither fear nor pity. I know what you cannot see. It is not pride that keeps me solitary. In your hands the honey of my mouth turns to poison. It is mere survival—yours and mine.

Change is eternity.

48

Becoming the Crocodile

IF YOU STAND ONLY ON the safety of the banks spearing fish, how can you know the depths of the river? Can you fathom the darkness under a ledge of rock or understand the life of the fish writhing on your spear? You mistake the teeth of the crocodile as the edge of the abyss, but the chasm is more terrible than teeth, and certain.

I fulfill the law and the law demands your blood. I am Sebak the crocodile, the catastrophe, the devourer, the necessity. Impaled on my teeth, you shall be blessed for you will glimpse truth. I am only the secrets of your own dark heart, your lust, your greed, your anger, your flesh. As long as you breathe, I shall exist to snatch you from yourself, to grind your bones and chew your flesh, to tear the darkness from your heart. I am the living power of water, the cry that catches in the throat, the sob that shatters stone.

On my teeth you smell the stink of flesh. To you I seem a living horror. But I tell you in truth, I am your own soul and it is with great sorrow that I crush the life you have made. I weep with the loss, but you do not believe. Such destruction is madness you say. You do not understand. Is it madness to cut the wheat so that bread can be made? When you were born into this bright land, did you not weep for the lost dark of the womb? Whether or not you understand the law, you exist because of it.

When you've reached the lips of the great devourer, you are staring into the jaws of creation.

Becoming the Heron

A THOUSAND LIVES I LIVED beneath the hand of the slaughterer—sacrificial ox, deer, lamb. Many times blessed by the knife, I rise from the block a new man, old discomforts of the heart cut away, new life throbbing like red, fresh blood. I know the power of the blade held at the throat, or paused above tangled locks of hair. I am bound by life for death, a turning beneath the clear sky. Here . . . the sting of the knife, the stroke of madness. Osiris wakes from a dream of earth.

I am the song, the witness, an old man resting on love like shining, slender blades of grass. I live an emerald moment. I change. Like a black jackal on a dark night, I am stealth. I've made a quiet passage to heaven. I've searched for secrets among colored stones. I am a blue heron, pure as bone. I know the stirrings of the Nile, the source where the river rises overlapped by trees, where flamingos dip and wade, where the fish are plentiful. I fly beneath an arch of trees straight into the eye of heaven. I make a long journey amid mud houses, singing. I've paused content on the river bank and stayed to watch the transformation of butterflies.

I was given a name on earth and a place in heaven. And I remember the quiet coming of goddesses along the river, baskets of fish on their heads, faces shining, feet caked with mud. I've wandered into empty temples at night and looked on the rough stone faces of dying gods; and I've paused with wonder at the entrance of shallow caves where the god-seekers smile and wait, clothed only in their own light. I know the cool mind of blue sky and the hot mysteries of earth. And I found my own gods while pecking seeds and resting on one leg watching reflections float on water.

Talk is unnecessary. We've been seduced by many words, many colors, many thorns, many bright flowers. I speak for the quiet language of sun, the yawn and shudder of a newborn lion covered with black markings. I speak for the gods hidden in things that cry: Uncover your faces. Through your own light, come. There is fire within you three thousand times over that you do not yet know. From your own bodies you give birth to all time and its seasons. The god you seek is within. The truth you chase lies between your own eyebrows. Look again with a different eye.

I am a blue heron, the messenger, a reborn and dying god. I celebrate neither birth nor death. Whatever is given me, I take like a fish from the water. By day I exist because I exist. By night I sail above the river, a single star wise in the darkness.

50

Becoming the Phoenix

I FLEW STRAIGHT OUT OF HEAVEN, a mad bird full of secrets. I came into being as I came into being. I grew as I grew. I changed as I change. My mind is fire, my soul fire. The cobra wakes and spits fire in my eyes. I rise through ochre smoke into black air enclosed in a shower of stars. I am what I have made. I am the seed of every god, beautiful as evening, hard as light. I am the last four days of yesterday, four screams from the edges of earth—beauty, terror, truth, madness—the phoenix on his pyre.

In a willow I made my nest of flowers and snakes, sandalwood and myrrh. I am waiting for eternity. I'm waiting for four hundred years to pass before I dance on flame, turn this desert to ash, before I rise, waking from gold and purple dreams into the season of god. I will live forever in the fire spun from my own wings. I'll suffer burns that burn to heal. I destroy and create myself like the sun that rises burning from the east and dies burning in the west. To know the fire, I become the fire. I am power. I am light. I am forever. On earth and in heaven I am. This is my body, my work. This is my deliverance.

The heat of transformation is unbearable, yet change is necessary. It burns up the useless, the diseased. Time is a cool liquid; it flows away like a river. We shall see no end of it.

Generation after generation, I create myself. It is never easy. Long nights I waited, lost in myself, considering the stars. I wage a battle against darkness, against my own ignorance, my resistance to change, my sentimental love for my own folly. Perfection is a difficult task. I lose and find my way over again. One task done gives rise to others. There is no end to the work left to do. That is harsh eternity. There is no end to becoming. I live forever striving for perfection. I praise the moment I die in fire for the veils of illusion burn with me. I see how hard we strive for truth, and once attained, how easily we forget it. I hold that fire as long as I can. My nose fills with the smell of seared flesh, the acrid smoke of death, so that years from now I might look on that scar and remember how it was to hold the light, how it was to die and come again radiant as light walking on sand.

I change and change again, generation after generation. I find anguish then peace.

I am satisfied with my birth and the fate to which it led me. I do not regret the discomforts and terrors of my mortality any more than I regret the company of angels. I have entered fire. I become invisible; yet I breathe in the flow of sun, in the eyes of children, in the light that animates the white cliffs at dawn. I am the god in the world in everything, even in darkness. If you have not seen me there, you have not looked. I am the fire that burns you, that burns in you. To live is to die a thousand deaths, but there is only one fire, one eternity.

51

Becoming a Light in the Darkness

OUT OF NOTHING I RETURN to the white sea foam. I have made an end of things. This is my last concern. I've held the striped pebble of love in my hand. I've smelled truth in the rain. Beyond lies light no darkness knows. I walk to it, through years of pain, lifetimes of suffering, despair that knew no comfort.

I've known that tempting feast of death when, while darkness filled the mind, the heart cried out. I know when the eye of truth is plucked from the head, only the blood of rage remains. I've known weakness and madness of the heart, the loneliness of travelers at night who came only near the fire to sleep. There are men grown weary and old among us, lost in their going; their heavy feet tramp the floor, passing in and out among the houses, going nowhere. I know the terrible truth of darkness, and I say, bless the darkness, for in darkness I stumbled and fell on the crystal road. After years of doubt, the dark mind turns again to light. In the black mountain of the heart, I found my way home again. I am that light in the darkness. I am a diamond, a bright secret veiled in black cloth. The light beyond heaven is the light within.

From the first cry to the last I chant the spell of living. In my belly I join the breath of life with the flame of becoming. I rise from the center of myself, fire on the wick, burning, tossing back shadows. Night drifts away like smoke. Yellow sunfish slice through the water flowing through the caverns of mountains toward the valley where fire begins. I worship at the altar of being. I offer up life in return for life, pleasure for pleasure, light for light. It is good to rest in the fire.

I remember the perfume of days, a flower unfurling slowly after a night of anguish. I remember the grapes I shared by the road with a stranger, and after the harvest, twenty black ibis pecking. I've found strength in the handle of a hoe, in the warmth of a woman's brown thigh. These simple graces are the light from which darkness flows away. I walk under a fragmented sky thinking how like a white god is the moon that sometimes walks with us, how the ashes of ancients rise again as children, how unseen music follows everywhere.

Each morning is like the first when bright gods rose and walked—a light passing between houses—into the flowering orchards. I am a feather through which light passes. Like the body of sky, I am filled with light. Like a spade that breaks the ground and prepares it, I enter the work of light. Like an old man on the last day or a child on the first, I wake from dark dreams. The mist of time disperses.

I hold in my hands the vulture and snake, the dying and the self-created. I take hold of the god within and learn the power of destiny. Beautiful are my hands and feet. Truth is in the belly. Before me lie the emerald days strung upon a gold string. Turquoise and crystal are the months. The heart and mind make peace in the body. I walk beneath a sky of lapis lazuli. How far I've travelled bruising my heels on stones, picking flowers, dreaming, telling stories. I spend my life amid the turnings of fate. At the end of day, I am a child with my basket full of fish, tired and happy on the streets, going home. I am light heading for light.

Even in the dark, a fire burns in the distance. Long years the hearth-keeper keeps his silence, lightening the dark, leading children home. There is food for the hungry, rest for the weary. Warm and light is the fire. Along the road, life's children sing. Voices join in the darkness. This is a beginning.

I have known terrors in the night, eaters of flesh, the teeth of evil. I have known anger and hatred, more terrible even by day because they were unexpected. And I learned to relax in the jaws of death, to relax my grasp on ruby life and let the world go on. I find joy in the advent of stars, in the song rising out of darkness. My heart fills with the spirit of wind, a great sail that carried the body home. I have heard the screams of my brothers lost in the darkness; they weep and cover their faces.

Lift your heads, throw down your hands and weep no more. The eye of creation looks upon you. Look back. You are crystal reflecting fire. In your own becoming there is light—enough to lead you home.

52

The Apes of Dawn

ACROSS THE RIVER THE APES GATHER, sitting quietly on their haunches, facing east, waiting for dawn. It is not yet light; a mist hangs above the river and the air is gray. They murmur and scratch themselves awake. First light breaks. A thin beam flies toward the hilltop and each animal raises his palms. Light slides through his fingers. He clutches air. Then the chorus begins.

A wise man wakes thus each morning, piercing his heart with light, empowering himself through the day. Swallows rise and dip above the river. The empty shells of trees and houses fill with color. The soul enters the body. The curtain of serpents parts. Time stands still, then rolls backwards. It is the first day.

You were once that innocent—a babe shrugging off the sleep of the womb, wailing for the moon, reaching toward light. We veil ourselves in the world's illusion; we learn how to forget.

I join the apes on the hill, facing east on my haunches. Quick light tumbles the wall of night. We raise our arms and howl. We summon the disk to appear and soon the sun crests the hill. In one moment the world has changed. We sing loudly of what we have seen. We tremble, mouths filled with light. Our song rings through eternity.

In the village below the people leave their houses, yawn, scratch and look about. "See!" one shouts. "There's that old fool with the apes again." The people stir and shake off sleep. We shout and keep shouting—the apes and me—until one by one we've awakened all those who otherwise would sleep through miracles.

The Heart of Carnelian

MINE IS A HEART OF carnelian, crimson as murder on a holy day. Mine is a heart of cornel, the gnarled roots of a dogwood and the bursting of flowers. I am the broken wax seal on my lover's letters. I am the red quartz in the deepest of mines. I am the phoenix, the fiery sun, consuming and resuming myself. I pace the halls of the underworld. I knock on the doors of death. I wander into the fields to stare at the sun and lie in the grass, ripe as a fig. The souls of the gods are with me. They hum like flies in my ears. I am I. I will what I will. Mine is a heart of carnelian, blood red as the crest of a phoenix.

The Cloth of Life

I AM BOUND IN THE cloth of life, wound about by magic. My sandals brush the carpet of Egypt. The words I speak bind my lips. What I fashion with these hands becomes me. Oh! the beauty I've beheld and the terror blind me like weights of gold. I am oversoothed by incense and myrrh. I lie too still on my comfortable bed. Hear the ducks squawk in the yard, the cattle bellow, the pigs snuffling air. See the herb's tender shoots, stalks of papyrus in a damp, green field. Taste the pumpkin and corn in the garden, the honied figs and wine, the joints of meat. Take them away. I walk in the procession of kings. Wisdom is my land, truth my breakfast.

I take this life, the man of clay wrapped in cloth, roll it up and tie it and bury it. Leave the field unplowed and my donkey free. I have no need of these. Unbound I am. What small matters I remember—things and their histories—shall be found in books by others. But the greater things—knowledge, goodness, love—shall flourish in my children's children. The sun will weave gold threads about them, dreams. They shall call this mantle life. I am with them everywhere, in the heart of god. This spirit touches all things—the illusion and the truth of matter in time.

The Knot of Isis

AT THE ENDS OF THE universe is a blood red cord that ties life to death, man to woman, will to destiny. Let the knot of that red sash, which cradles the hips of the goddess, bind in me the ends of life and dream. I'm an old man with more than my share of hopes and misgivings. Let my thoughts lie together in peace. At my death let the bubbles of blood on my lips taste as sweet as berries. Give me not words of consolation. Give me magic, the fire of one beyond the borders of enchantment. Give me the spell of living well.

Do I lie on the floor of my house or within the temple? Is the hand that soothes me that of wife or priestess? I rise and walk. The sky arcs ever around; the world spreads itself beneath my feet. We are bound mind to Mind, heart to Heart—no difference rises between the shadow of my footsteps and the will of god. I walk in harmony, heaven in one hand, earth in the other. I am the knot where two worlds meet. Red magic courses through me like the blood of Isis, magic of magic, spirit of spirit. I am proof of the power of gods. I am water and dust walking.

56

The Pillow of Hands

I REST UPON THE PILLOW of heaven, the cradled hands of my father. I lift my head; my mouth fills with words and wonder. Stars explode into being. The wind pulses through the valley—the hot heart and breath of god. I am flesh of my father's flesh. His sorrows are mine, his joys, his spirit. I rest on the pillow of his hands. The fallen shall rise and the uprisen shall fall. He shall comfort them. Sleepers wake and the awakened forget; such rhythm is the restless tide. I rise gently, fall softly. There is no struggle, no more tormented dream on the pillow of his hands, Oh Osiris.

Column of Gold

BESIDE THE WELL THE SYCAMORE RISES. Beside the well bright cornflowers grow. Do they rise on their tender stalks by will or does some force of love mold them, drive them up? In the seed lies the will to become and the greater will gives form. The power of the green shoot parts the earth. The water in the well is nourishing.

I rise. My spine is of bone, sinew and flesh. I am a man desirous of life. I will dance, harvest corn and make children. I will make my peace with earth. I shine. The power of gods courses through me and makes of my backbone a column of gold. I am the flower on its stalk, the budding of sycamore branches. I am the pillar on which the balance of life is weighed. Oh! my heart beats with joy; my life is golden as the humming of bees.

I live for a time and pass away, but the column of gold will stand. The powers of gods shape us, and those who give themselves not to its will, grow twisted, bent and stunted. It is easier to live in the light of the great will, to love than to grow in the shadows of self imaginings. As the gods will, so grows the universe.

I rise.

I am a column of gold, eternal, at peace, in harmony.

58

The Eye of God

THE EYE OPENS SEEING OLD MEN, women and children. The eye opens seeing gods, flesh, vapors. The eye recalls the beauty of the ordinary. It sees me, therefore I am. As such are we all created. It watches and pierces the heart. Who knows its name? Call it love, creation, conspiracy. Call it an impossible sky hung with moons and stars. It is yesterday or tomorrow, a million years travelling. The sun circles and the hawk. We follow a flow. Thus looked upon the world receives its god.

I lived in the delta in a house of mud when I first felt its glance. I lived in its fire and never knew. I was asleep, dreaming blue dreams in the egg of the world. The eye opened and closed, blinking once perhaps as it does every million years, and I came from unknowing into knowing. I left my hut yawning. I was naked in a bed of light. I shone like day. I opened like a purple flower at dawn.

I am in the eye of god, resting in its blue orb. Golden eyelids encircle me. Eyelashes grow like stalks of dark truth. I see what I never dared— beyond the bucket banging the well, beyond mountains pushing up dirt. Light shimmers in every blade of grass, gods dance in every leaf, blue and gold fires leap from my pores. I shine in and out of life.

A thousand forms have I, wholly mine—man and hawk, sycamore, lotus and fig. I please myself to be born and to die over again. I walk a flowered path bordered by a million years. Season to season I change as a leaf greening. I flow as blood through flesh. The eye opens and closes, and then . . .

What lives in the gods and rivers lives in me, parts of the whole, one in One. I take my journey seriously. I've seen mountains, deserts and seas. Going nowhere one morning I suddenly entered heaven. I opened its door and passed through. I stood on polished floors and understood heaven no better there than while I was planting corn. Then I laughed; in that was truth.

Does the world die with me when I sleep? It seems so. I wake in the morning and it is born again—my wife, my children, my cattle, the stars. There are times in the day when I forget her, then seeing her pass, a jug of water on one hip, she is born in me and love rises.

All things are one beheld in the eye of god. We are his bodies. His time moves in our bellies. There is no season in which heaven does not hold the shape of its beloved, no time in which the earth does not sing. Under the sun, flamingos nod and bow and walk. Birds of the air spin in countless exhaled breaths. We are growing, remembering, forgetting, becoming. The many are one face changing expression.

The eye is everywhere. There is no act it does not see, no desire it cannot hold, no secret that cannot be known. The heavens speak. The flame bursts on your cheeks. Things are possible. In a moment we live a million years, a thousand lives in a breath.

Behold the eye that holds you. Without hands, it made you. You will be its hands. Without tongue, you become its tongue. Your work is its will. If what you make—your body, your love, your peace—is good, it shall be looked on by gods and endure forever.

When the eye opens, I look back.

59

Entering the House

THERE IS A HOUSE BUILT for me on the rocks above the river where the odor of sweet roots and flowers keeps goats and gods company. To reach it I walked through papyrus marshes, spikelets of flowers towering. I rested shaded by tall reeds and watched a hawk in flight. Through this journey it followed me like a beautiful wife, now crying, now singing. I plowed blue fields of flax, wove flowers into robes, crushed seeds to make oil. I have been many men in my passage and as often as I thought of death, I thought of my palm grove. All my life goats danced upon these hills. All my life I've seen the same spring, different goats amid different flowers.

In the house there is meat for the hungry. There is truth for those who can hear. At night around the house lie a thousand stars. The world's infinite arms carry the weary home.

My bread is made of white corn. My beer is made of red barley. Hungrily I eat the gods' food and join a feast of mystery. Along the river, barges filled with grain and cake and ale pass. Gods reside with sailors and farmers. Blessed are those who feed the people. Beneath fruit trees I ponder blossoms and tassels. Like the slender arms of dancing women are their hanging branches. I lie on my back and shudder to think it might be some vaporous dream. It is good to be here, a husband of earth.

No greater joy exists than a walk among gardens, smelling herbs and flowers. I am lifted from the fretful earth as the green plant lifts clods of dirt. The sun pours its grace upon my head, its luster an oil falling from a red jar. This is the house where spirit was born. My bones and skin I leave like rags. I tear the veil and see the light I am. I feast on the silence of gods and the reticence of the world. Like smoke, like prayers I am lifted up. Beauty is. All things are possible.

Across the sky, gods and goddesses pass. Fire and air, spirit and light. What we imagine comes to pass. Thought finds its form. All forgotten things return. This moment marks a time. I endure the ages. My heart contains all I am, all flood of love, all thoughts invisible and vital as air.

I leave the fields and enter the house. The journey ends there. I am a man returning home. Welcomed by family, embraced by ancestors, I am again that which I was, a soul, a fire clothed in heaven, a sparrow. Born of stars, I am a god naming the life that was always mine.

Long tables are stacked with cakes. The scent of sandalwood rises. The house fills with birds and the smell of beer and ale. I enter the circle of sun. I speak with priests and hermits. I know words that draw light into the darkness. I know the vulture and the carcass. I know the eggs in the nest. I am a silver star hanging above the world, courage in the blackest night. I am swift water running, a lowing cow, the thought of myself in my father's forehead.

I stand in peace before the world. I nourish and am nourished by love. Like a lotus, quiet upon the water, I listen and repeat the silence. I am Osiris: man and god, black obsidian reflecting light.

60

Entering Truth

ONE AFTERNOON AS GRAPES WERE ripening and I stood in my field, I heard death fingering his lyre among the wheat. Eight was the number of his song, eight gods, one note dividing, harmony returning. I laid aside my work, gathering what I knew and loved. Clothed in the skin of a priest, I hurried toward light bearing the light within. Toward the unknown world I bore the world I had known. Then came the floods, the wind storms and the fire, and the solid earth shook itself into a thousand pieces. All I thought was mine was driven from me. I entered darkness. I entered stone. Naked, I entered truth. No fragrant cedar tree grew there. Acacia trees sent forth no shoots. No figs ripened, no honey dripped from the trees, no fragrant boughs soothed. Neither herbs nor grasses clung to the ground. I was awed, afraid to enter the place of hidden things. Without eyes or ears or tongue or flesh, I was nothing, possessing nothing. I came across the desert through shifting sands, driving wind and mirage to meet my god.

With me stood a thousand others called from their fields, from their kilns, from their boats, their lovers' arms. Some cowered, some hid in the mask of their hands. Others swooned. They clung to each other trembling. I raised my arms and spoke with the night. Darkness gathered—I could not see my own hand, the night so thick I could not feel my own skin. Like clouds in the wind or the pattern of weather, the crowd dispersed and I stood alone.

A star trembled in the empty air like the winking eye of god. Closer it drew, brightening, directing its light on me. In that light I saw a throng of others, glimmering like countless stars, dimming then growing bright—men and women, children passing, walking before me, growing young then old, turning into bones, then into dust, then into swirling lights. I saw men become women, snakes become birds, cattle become stone, skeletons become children. I saw them couple and I saw them dance. I saw worms writhe in their bellies. They sang and cried. They laughed and were silent. I looked in their hearts and saw their secrets. Their countless thoughts and dreams filled me. As they walked, each passed through me and I shivered. I knew their stories better than my own, recalled their pleasures and sorrows, their failures and moments of grace. And as they marched on in infinity like a thousand bodies streaming from one body of sky, I saw the gate from which they had flooded lay open. I entered into truth.

Thick winds blew the torrid air across an expanse of sand. A multitude of lights fluttered, becoming birds: hawks, swallows, herons, ibis, geese, flamingo, quail, vultures, lapwings, sparrow and owls. They stormed my head, calling to each other, then settled in the branches of a sycamore. They cocked their glittering eyes. I waited. Soon the jackal came, sniffing at my belly, tearing at my flesh. My arms and hair filled his teeth. I let him make his meal of me. My heart he tore out, pawed and sniffed, then turned it over, thinking, weighing his words.

"Beyond skin or meat or bones," he said, "beyond blood or hair or humors, he is one of us. His odor is as calamus, sweet as frankincense. He is fragrant as a god. From far fields he passed through towns, crossing the river, winding under date palms. Long years he passed through wind and fire. He walked upon the flood waters. His journey is marked by sorrow and joy. His triumphs are etched in his heart. He is an old man come in peace with a story."

The birds in the tree nodded looking one to the other. For a long time I stood listening to the hot winds shuffling sand. "Speak," said the jackal, and this I said:

I stand before the mirror looking back in time. I was born a man. Before that I was a god. I was with you when time began. I've not denied you. To do so would be to deny myself. Because I delight in fresh bread, the smell of clover and the thighs of women, I live; therefore, you live with me. We are the same—more than brothers. We are one heart, one fire.

I was a man of Egypt, born of woman on a sheet of linen in a green valley rent by a river between two worlds of sand. I was earth in the hands of the potter who gathered me, who molded me in fire and air, who made me a child and gave me to my mother, a poor woman and a goddess. She suckled me, gave me the power of words. I was healthy and sick, prosperous and poor. I learned hope and regret. When I was a man I was given my own children—such delicate gods it broke my heart. I cradled their heads, brushed the down on their cheeks with my fingers, gave them bread to eat. Some I buried before me and wept bitter tears. Then I grew old and my children grew strong. I was a grandfather many times.

I was a man of Egypt going to the river often to behold the gods who dwell in the rushes, who dwell in the frogs and in the heron. In my hands I held the divinity of colored stones, and in time I learned to handle the delicate hearts of men. By discovering fragrant cedars, date palms and eagles, I discovered life. I burned incense in the temples, but offered only myself for nothing else was mine to give.

I've known the charms of sycamore trees, children hanging apelike from sturdy branches, or passing clouds snatched for a moment by green leaves, or cattle lowing in the shade. And I know the lifeless sand that forms after the tree is gone. To the trees I made offerings of water. In this way I paid homage to gods. I plowed my fields. I milked my goats and cows. I took care of my wife and mother. I danced with my daughter, made friends with fishermen. I saw beggars with outstretched arms gathering at the river. I saw rats run between the feet of children. I saw strong women hauling water in the red flag of evening. I saw priests and judges bathing in the rushes. I saw crocodiles slip silently from the bank. I saw houses of mud and white cities glittering beneath date palms. I saw fields of wheat, grapes and cotton. I saw fish floundering in nets and donkeys steaming in the river. And I was full of wonder.

On the water many afternoons I fell to silent dreaming. I wandered the valley, the mountains and desert searching for the sun's end, but discovered more secrets and travelled more ground in the arms and hips of women. I fought those who would have harmed my children. I threw an ax in the face of evil. I did what I thought was right. When the oxen were tired I let them rest. When the children were hungry I gave them bread and honey. Where the statues of gods were overturned I set them back on their pedestals. And when, after so much effort, my plans went awry I acquiesced to a greater authority.

Then one day, laden with flowers and lamb and cake, I visited the tomb of an uncle and found myself lying there among the spices and linen. That is how I left the garden. That is how I entered the heart of the mountain. I had wondrous dreams of bright hawks soaring through dark corridors. At the well I met a blind woman who called me "son." In the temples I stood so long the priests gathered, asking, "What brings a man so far to sit and stare into the air?"

"I want to see beyond the veil."

"Go back to your fields, old man. There are no secrets here." They laughed and left me to thought.

For several years I came and went in the temples, praising the gods, staring into the faces of their statues. Then one afternoon—I don't know why, perhaps the sun shone on me—a priest led me to the room of secrets. I saw a young girl spinning strands of flax and an old woman baking raisin cakes. Through a window I saw a man plowing his field, struggling to upturn a stone and calling to his stubborn donkeys. A hawk circled overhead, while two children tossed a small fish back into the river.

I moved to speak, but the priest held up his hand. "You must be silent now. You are staring into the face of god."

And I wept with joy. Though I'd seen my life before, that moment I knew it differently. From then on I sowed barley and walked under trees with wonder. I stumbled once and fell, then sat laughing in the road. Two boys rushed from their houses to uplift me.

"Old man, where do you live?" they asked. "We will carry you home."

I stretched out my arms, flinging them north and south, east and west. "Here," I said. "In the house of perpetuity!"

One day I died and was wound about with linen, myrrh and gum. My wife wept and my children sang. They poured spices and tears over my chest. The village men circled me with earth. They lay copper necklaces in my tomb, returning precious earth to earth. Left in the mountain for some days, I rose and uncovered myself, shedding skins like a snake. I was naked and new. I left bones and rags hidden in the dirt and I walked the corridor toward light.

There I came to this desert. Before me a thousand souls rose from the sand like gods. Together we walked the wasteland, together we crossed the bitter lakes. Naked we entered Truth. I stand before you now, having seen the ghosts of the long dead and the unborn, having seen skeletons and children, having seen blue starlight filter through the outstretched wings of a bird. Before you I stand a whole man speaking. I made a long journey. I did what I thought was right. I have come to see the gods.

Then rose the snake from the sand and coiled about my ankle hissing. "Fantasies all. What gives you the right to make demands of the gods?"

"I speak in truth," I said. "Not to humor you. Dead men have no need of pretense. What I seek is truth, light beyond light beyond Light. There are those who will tell you a different story. Who is to say which is right? But this I know: what I've seen with the eye has been fantasy, perhaps; but what I've known with the heart has been truth."

The snake observed me with amber eyes. He motioned toward a door that opened from air into air. "If that is so, can your heart name the name of this gate?"

"Being," I said.

"And the lands on either side?"

"Creation and destruction."

151

"Pass then, Osiris," he said.

The snake withdrew and the multicolored birds gathered, circling in the dark, gathering me, lifting me up. I stepped through and nothing changed, yet I had entered heaven. Still myself alone on the desert at night, I walked while winds scoured the sand below and in the distance a jackal howled at the stars.

61

The Confession

IN EVERY STONE THE GODS live, in the bushes, in the eyes of children. In every stone lies truth one could hold in the hand. In every breath we speak what we know, being what we are. I am a man of good intention. I know a god or crocodile when I see one. I know the branches that make the tree. I know the sap that rises and falls and the fidelity from which blossoms spring. And I've heard of horrors awaiting men who never see the action of gods in things. I've heard talk of blood and sinew, but I know worse than this must be the shock of falling from earth, of becoming less than a gnat flung from the hand of god. It is not death I fear, it is unbeing and uselessness, of having never been.

I am a man given mostly to song, to pleasantries and not to fact. I've been too eager to congratulate myself. Confessions never come easily. Today I put aside the lyre and hold the stone of truth. Today I repeat what gods know.

I've told stories for the delight of story, but where truth was needed I told no lie. Though never easy, I turned from easy profit. When the cow ran, I ran after the cow. Whether I stood before children, men or gods, I've not given myself airs. Harder still, I've not mocked those who did.

I've spoken the names of the gods daily that they might live in me. I have not asked them to do that of which I am able. I've done their will when requested. When they gave me strength, I gave them the profit of strength. Through too much talk I've learned wisdom is silent. I've caused no servant to be whipped by his master. I broke no woman's heart. I gave my wife laughter instead of tears. I took no man's life in word or deed.

I stole no milk from the mouths of children nor the temple ale and cake. I've taken no riches from the dead, other than the words by which they taught me. I stole neither grapes nor figs from my neighbor's orchard. I tramped not on the wheat in his field. When we had food, I fed beggars and priests; when we had but kernels, I fed the children. When the time came, I gave the king his due, though I had but little. When others had little and I had much, I gave the king his corn and shared with my neighbors.

I made love to my wife. We raised fine sons and daughters. We shared our bodies like a secret. When another's wife offered herself to me, I spent the afternoon plowing. When starved cattle came to my pasture, I did not chase them away. I killed no bird soaring above the cliffs, nor captured ducks on the public river. I caught only the fish our mouths could eat. I baited no hook nor deceived them with meat. When the floods came even to the floors of my house, I gave them my fields and turned water from no man. Where once there was desert, I irrigated the land and wheat grew. The flowers that grew wild, I let grow.

I have not hurried a difficult day by praying for night. I extinguished no candle before its hour. I have not tested the limits imposed by gods nor tried to turn back the stampede of events that brought me to my knees and destiny. In all things—the opening of cornflowers, the opening of my heart—I've seen the hand of god.

Of these things I am pleased, but pride brings grief when proclaimed too loudly. Though I lay with no other woman I often imagined it so. I diverted attention from my wife. Not often enough did I praise her work or kiss the bread dough from her fingers. Not often enough did I hold and pet my children. Not often enough was I silent in the temple of the world. Not often did I listen well when an old man told his story.

I have been tired and stopped short in my journey when I could have travelled further. I broke the bowl rather than wash it. I blamed the goat for rancid cheese. Many times in life I longed for death and despised the gift of gods. I've been angry, impatient and afraid. In ignorance I failed to see light gathering. Consumed with sorrow, I ignored the sorrows of others. Too often I judged the actions of friends, too often closed my eyes to the injustice of others. I've thought too much and done too little. I longed to take care of the world when I should have taken care of my family.

Not a perfect soul, I am perfecting. Not human being, I am human becoming. A phoenix asleep in the ashes of night, I rise anew each day. I burn with fever, with all I crave to know. I enter the temple, my mind afire. I've come to burn down the house.

Gods live not in the crevices of mortar and stone, nor in the jeweled eyes of a ram but in the hands of men and the hearts of women and in the land of wonder. Dip your cup in the river and you drink in gods. Breathe the air and gods fly up your nose. The god in the wind puffs the sail and speeds the traveler home. Nodding and crowing, the lapwings are gods clinging to sycamore branches. Daily gods rise in blades of wheat. Daily they walk cities by the river. Covered with the blood and mucus of women, gods enter the world and we call them children.

To see the goodness of things, we must see the god in things. To see the god in things, we must see goodness. To find god in sorrow, fear and death is to see its usefulness. To know is to understand. To praise the gods, we must praise life. To honor gods we must make of the world something good. To be gods, we must hold goodness in each pore. We are filled with light, wholly divine. The sun rises, an eye of fire, and through its light we come to see the world as gods would have it.

In the land of the sun, in the season of the end, I climb the highest hill. The moon is a sliver caught in the trees. Entering night I carry the lamp. Though no man sees it, I shine my light into darkness. See how even a single beam cuts through so the path lies clear. The wolves run frightened. Still, no great harm comes to a man who walks unafraid to die.

I leave these words to those with ears to hear, eyes to see, hearts to know, hands to do. I leave these words in the world of forms. I am becoming invisible.

I speak the names of gods and so saying, my words give power and life. Their power gives truth light as a feather, a soul light as air.

Hail long-legged beast striding through the cornfield, creature from the house of light, I've seen nothing in the world but beauty. May we live forever.

Hail priest of incense, smoke and flame, fresh from the soul's daily battle, I've taken nothing from life but strength. May we live forever.

Hail wind in my face blown from the mouths of gods, I returned the goslings to their nest. The hawks soar freely above the cliffs. May we live forever.

Hail devourer of shadows, terror lurking in the entrails of mountains, I extinguished no man's light. I took neither his life nor dreams. May we live forever.

Hail that which brings the trees to flower, the wheat to grow, the lotus to blossom, which bursts from the black bowels of earth singing, I've not wasted the gift of your labors. May we live forever.

Hail lion of heaven, bearer of yesterday and tomorrow, I've not been less than what I was. May we live forever.

Hail seamstress of the cloth of life, whose thread is gold, whose needles are fire, I've not severed the cord that binds men to their gods and destiny. May we live forever.

Hail candle guttering in the wind, flame that lashes like the blown branches of trees, my resolve wavered, but my spirit was never broken. May we endure forever.

Hail crocodile, crusher of bones hiding in the rushes of the river, I am not afraid. May we live forever.

Hail tongue of fire spit from the mouth of a god, hail word that took root in the desert. Hail craftsman of forms, utterer of life, I've told no lies. May we live forever.

Hail two pairs of lips touching in the amber blush of sunset, I've not wasted love. May we live forever.

Hail fair of face hidden among the flowers, sudden snake entwined around blossoms, I've not made my wife blind with tears. May we live forever.

Hail peaceful cat stretched out in the noonday sun, warm and content and asleep, I've not made myself so unhappy with plans and foolish insistences that I could not find pleasure in the hour. May we live forever.

Hail star in the darkness, white spider legs dancing on a web of night, I've made my home within. Wherever I go, I am no stranger. May we live forever.

Hail spitter of my blood coming back from the slaughter, I never shrank from the task. May we live forever.

Hail claw in my heart, talon of the hawk, knife in my gut, I gave no man poison and called it nectar, but the bitter herb I drank killed and cleansed and freed me. I am new. May we live forever.

Hail listener in the dark, I've not troubled myself with the small words men say. I hear the words gods weave into silence. May we live forever.

Hail odd one walking backwards with grace, who am I to say otherwise? May we live forever.

Hail bull inflamed with the heat of the sun, I took the blow and gave no cause for rage. May we live forever.

Hail head of the serpent, beauty, terror and grace, hypnotic yellow eye, I danced with an old man's young wife as he tended his garden. I spoke with her while my wife fed our children. She was like a well of sweet water that begged to be lifted up. I hurried home. I defiled the woman of no man, but god, how I thought of it. May we all live forever.

Hail seer of the beginning and the end coming forth unbidden, I've not altered the flow of nature. I released myself to destiny. A seed must take root. Winds must blow. May we live forever.

Hail great face beyond the sky, looking down on men, a falcon crowns the sycamore and I walk in its shadow. There are days I feel like climbing up to heaven. May we live forever.

Hail river that swells its banks, heart overflowing, I've not run from the flood. May we live forever.

Hail breath of god, throat of the goddess, I've not wasted my time with harsh words. May we live forever.

Hail child rising like a lotus from the river, I've heard the seductive song of reason. I know the truth in my belly. May we live forever.

Hail god of gods, web of being, I've not ensnared myself in my own sorrow. May we live forever.

Hail peace that comes of its own volition, I've not chased after things I thought would make me happy. May we live forever.

Hail fortune teller, portent of things to come, I have followed my instincts. Though I sought the counsel of others, I have not let their words stir confusion. May we live forever.

Hail three faces: truth, doubt and expedience coming out of the snake's milky mouth, I've not gone back upon my word. May we live forever.

Hail wise man sitting by the river listening to birds, I've strained to hear the secrets of my own heart rather than the thoughts of another. May we live forever.

Hail two plumes of the ostrich, two horns of the ram, I've not wasted time talking while my hands slept in my lap. May we live forever.

Hail beginning and end, sunrise and sunset, I've not wasted light trying to reveal another's inconsistencies. May we live forever.

Hail smoking sun, burner of the mists of time, straight of spine, order sprung from chaos, I've not encircled other men with curses. May we live forever.

Hail seer into hearts, I have walked the burning sands, seen my crops destroyed and lost my sheep to jackals; but I've not ruined the good taste of my wife's bread worrying with these troubles. May we live forever.

Hail herald of kings on a barge brightly covered with flags, I've not proclaimed myself. May we live forever.

Hail vulture upon the sycamore branch, I've not made false promises or hasty oaths. I've not bound myself to the gods with a lesser magic than love. May we live forever.

Hail snake in the grass near his snake hole by the river, I've not searched for a crack in every pot. May we live forever.

Hail gold hawk spinning charms above the caves in the cliffs, I've not tried to darken the light of the moon. I've not looked for mold on the bread of gods. All things are perfect in themselves. May we live forever.

Hail mind of heaven, arranger of the stars, I've not questioned the laws of nature, nor scorned the gods of another man. May we live in peace forever.

Hail hands of fire, baker of bread and men and truth, I've not fed myself before the hungry child. I've not carried off the praise intended for gods. May we live forever.

Hail white teeth, a biter of heads, devourer of men, I have not killed the cow nor uprooted the wheat, but that I know its spirit feeds mine. When the time comes, I give up life without regret to feed a spirit greater than mine. I shall die, a small thing become part of the larger world. May we live forever and forever.

May the light shine through us and on us and in us. May we die each night and be born each morning that the wonder of life should not escape us. May we love and laugh and enter lightly into each other's hearts. May we live forever. May we live forever.

62

The Bath

MY MOUTH AND HANDS WERE green innocent seedlings, moments in time. "Come, come," the beautiful one said. I grew in grace under the eyes of gods. I thought I was content, but the cat drank sweet milk and the ass bore the burden in the house of cross purposes. My joy was mindless and I was afraid even of the shadows of passing clouds. I lived in the fear of loss. So, relinquishing comfort and ease I journeyed.

I have seen the broken-down boughs of the fig tree overladen with fruit. I have seen death dance over desert sands, his bone-white head turned behind. I have offered up saffron and myrrh to goddesses. I know the bread and honey that old men like. I have walked nine days in wonder down a long, dust-swept road just to say: You think you are awake, but you are asleep. When was the last day your heart leapt and cried, "I am alive in Egypt?" I stand poised in the fragrance of purple amaranth. I am a flower that never dies.

Lord of the winds, deliver me like a seed blown to fertile ground. What has become of the leopard's three spotted whelps who once played outside my door? Do their skins cover the hides of priests? Do their tails make fringe for the tax collector's wife's robe? Do the woman and the priest cover their faces when they parade their souls in town? Let our lives and deaths be toward some purpose. I smell a change coming, a shape turning leaves in the wind.

One night I went out under the cover of stars to the southern pool and bathed there among the lotus. My breast, my face, my buttocks, my feet I immersed in water and moonlight. I was silver, alive, no part of me untouched by beauty or dread. I rested. In the field of reeds that lay to the north, I heard grasshoppers chew the tender stalks and a thousand legs leapt into the silence as a snake slithered by, disturbing their feast. I saw, too, the luminous faces of the dead—sailors all—come quietly from the house of gods to bathe with mortals in the pool of lotus under a silver moon.

"We come night or day to this water of the spirit," they said. "It is good to feel again the liquid pleasure of earth."

"It is good," I answered and they were surprised for as many as they are and as often as they come, few men of earth ever see them. They gave me then a honied cake to eat that I, like them, might pass through the villages invisible and touch with my feet the floor of the gods' house in the sky. They gave me, too, a bitter cake that, when this night of spirits had long passed, I might eat again and remember.

"Who are you, brother?" they asked. "What is the secret name of your soul? From where do you get your power?"

I read the name etched on my heart. "I am the sweet-smelling flowers of the olive tree," I said.

"Come," they said and I took on the robe of night. We passed north of the towns through the rushes. And I saw through the windows of houses women bent in love above their husbands, old men staring into the dark, children dreaming of flying. "What do you see?" the sailors asked.

"I see flesh walking. I see souls sheathed in paper. I see the spirits of two children hovering above a woman in love, waiting to jump in her belly and be born. I see comfort and sorrow, rejoicing and forgetting. I am staring into the heart of Egypt."

Then the sailors reached into the air shimmering around them, pulled down a stylus of fire and a tablet of crystal. "Write it down," they said, and I wrote it down, and it seemed I was not so much recording what I had seen, but remembering what I already knew. Then they parted the bones of my chest with their hands and buried the tablet within my heart. As it touched me crystal words sprang to my lips. A message coursed through my veins and etched itself in the lines of my palm. I became fertile ground in which the shining ones planted seed, into which

I'd written my own destiny, taken on my own becoming, and that night began a new life.

The stylus of fire extinguished itself and its smoke curled through the air, a white ribbon weaving in and out of stars. We rose following it, like a flock of geese lifting easily off the surface of water, flying straight into heaven.

"Fly," they said, and we flew until we came to a great house in the sky made all of air. In it gods and goddesses were walking. They danced and sang, ate cakes, drank wine, and their laughter echoed through the night. And I knew I saw what, in the twinkling nights I had passed on earth, had seemed the quiet conversation of stars. I was amazed, struck dumb; and the sailors smiled. "This is the party you've waited for. The ways have been arranged. Call it eternal life, call it vibration. It lasts a million years. Go in. The gods wait for you."

I moved to enter and the hand of a god touched me. "This feast is for gods," he said. "Are you a god?"

I turned in confusion. I am no god, I thought. I am only a man who has spent most of his days behind the ass of a donkey and plow. I am but a sack of bones covered with skin and, often, mud. I have no right to feast with gods. Hot tears of shame scoured my cheeks and the shining ones laughed, slapping each other's backs.

"Have you forgotten so soon what you learned in the lotus pool? Try not thinking so much. Look at the words in your heart."

I looked and saw, and facing the guardian said, "I know you. I have seen you a thousand times. You are the bolt of heaven, the truth, flickering light of the morning star."

"Who am I?" called another and another and another and another.

Then I named them one by one. "You are laughter asleep in two jugs of red wine. You are the presence of gods on earth. And you, lady, are the white gazelle gracing earth, quick and beautiful. You are water bubbling out of the well. And you, you are the backbone of the sky. You are mother of birds, maker of nests, feeder of young, the soarer, the watcher. You are the blue eye of heaven, the gold knot of life. You are ether. You are the abyss, the mouth of the crocodile, the rose-colored mountain at dawn. You are the thoughts that gods see. You are the shadow, the shade of trees, the entrance of caves. You are wind, a lion walking in light. You are the arms of heaven. You are mistress of the house, a snake sleeping coiled in the water pot. You are mother and midwife and concubine. You are the sunfish darting between the reeds. You are the power of things alive, essence of flowers, of rams, of men. You are sorceress, mother of jackals, friend of sparrows, weeper of tears, singer of songs. You are my hands, my arms, my face, my feet. You are all parts of me. You live in my head and my heart and my belly."

And I crossed the threshold of the great house. The gods embraced me with joy and weeping. "It is good to have you here. No man comes home unless he knows in his soul who he is. You have lived too long away from us who are yourselves. The traveler Osiris, the son, the god is home."

Then I ate with them the bread of life and drank the wine of remembering. We danced and I was drunk with knowing and pleasure. I wore the white linen of a god. We danced until the walls of the great house burst into flame; the fire joined me to them, all to myself. I fell down and wept and when at last I opened my eyes, I saw before me my own face reflected on the surface of a pool of water.

I rose from my bath as the sun burst over the horizon. A new day had come. I had died in the night and been reborn. Then I dressed and walked the dusty path toward my house, thinking, "My wife will be waking now. She will wonder where I have been." And I thought with pleasure of the amazement on her face when I would answer her. "I was everywhere on heaven and earth with gods."

This Body of Light

I WAKE AS FROM A DREAM. "Come," he said. My heart opens, fills with light. My hair drips as if I rose new from the sea. Beads of crystal light surround me. I live a million years. Is my face radiant? Does it glow like the sun on the horizon? The god within shows himself, the soul walks out, the mind of fire burns. Are my eyes shining? Do you see in them beauty? Love? Are they filled with the radiance of sky—a gold sun, a silver moon? My ears are radiant. I know the silver song of day. I sing it. My heart opens, the door, the way. Are my lips shining? Do they dance over these words? Can you hear the name of light? A silver river snakes through dark mountains. Are my teeth pillars of alabaster? Words of truth pass over them. Words of magic burst in the air becoming swallows. I am filled with wonder and light. My tongue is the tongue of fire. My blood is the blood of Isis. Life grows through me. Love grows in me. It is dawn when the lotus flowers.

My hands radiate heat. I am a changeling, a man become god. Touch me. I burn with fever. With my hands I make visible thoughts. I create the world every day. My blazing fingers burn holes in the blanket of sky and the night is filled with stars. The cobra's fire lies coiled in my shoulders. Awake! My arms are snakes. I hold the plume and the knife. I encircle the world. Voices of the dead well up and all around the world flares in silence. My arms form the shuttle of the loom. Beams of sun are the gods' strands of gold. My thoughts are blue threads; the unformed words, spaces between. I weave the cloth of life. I wear its shining robe and live a million years.

Is my backbone straight, a column of fire thrown up from the peak of mountain? Do I rise like a flame dispelling night? Am I the wick, the center of fire? Does my heart burn within my chest? I am white with heat. I am a vessel ablaze in the kiln, made strong to hold love, hunger, sorrow. My flesh glows. Each pore of skin fills with light. My bones and intestines fill with light. The god light springs up all around. Even monkeys and snakes stare.

Is my navel the eye of Horus that having seen all from beginning to end, turns, blind to the outer world, and looks within? Can you see the embers of fire burn within my belly? My cock rises like a stalk of corn swelling with yellow seed. I reap a harvest beyond pleasure. New bodies dance in a stream of sunlight. Fire rolls out of me as the sun rolls from the hips of the sky, as a woman gives birth to her children. Through villages, orchards and burning desert, these legs carry me as my body carried eternity. My feet are afire with the power of travelling, arriving, departing, knowing each step.

Each moment the moment begins again. There is nothing I haven't seen—calm waters flowing over a thousand pebbles, the snake sunning upon a dry boulder, and the core of fire that cannot be concealed, washed away or broken, lighting each pebble from within. I am radiant as the points of stars in the ubiquitous heart of god.

The Family

WHAT DOES IT MEAN TO have come home, but to have entered the place where a man lives, to have pierced skin and found red desire that lingers, to know that love is salve and salvation. Family is all that the house may hold. Blessings on he who enters.

In that house laid out in a circle of rooms, gods and goddesses wove their magic, lighting tapers of beeswax and reading books. The glow of candles had bronzed their skin. I flow in as if in dream. A yellow leaf falls in the reflecting pool and shatters. The sounds of the gods' names are music.

"Enter me," cried Isis. "I shall make you god." Enchantress and wife, she stamps and spins. She raises her arms to dance. From her armpits rises a hot perfume that fills the sails of boats along the Nile. She stirs breezes that make the sailors swoon and opens the eyes of statues. Under her spell, I come to myself; under her body I come to life. Dawn breaks through the diaphanous weave of her dress. She dances and draws down heaven. Sparks scatter from her heels and on earth tumbles forth an expanse of stars. I take her arms. I taste her lips. I lose myself in beauty and chaos. To love is to believe in goddesses.

"Follow me," said Anubis. "We'll go a road few men have walked." In dark corridors we pass, a pair of jackals black as the black around us. We are beastly forms made beautiful in moonlight, beheld by gods, healed by gods' eyes, held up by the air streaming from their nostrils. Together we are twilight and dawn. I am the left eye and he is the right. Beneath the old man's eyebrows we make a fine sight, beholding things gods have made. The world is a body of light and its forehead a peaceful kingdom. Here we live in states of grace.

With three fingers I raise myself unto clouds. I ride the back of a mountain, and looking down see cities of stone, cities of clay, cities of clouds, cities unimaginable. I heard the words that shatter crystal. My language is shot through with the speech of gods. My tongue curls over words not my own. I am filled by the great god who walks fair paths, filling the roadside with song. Vultures pick at the flesh of a man fallen. Flowers grow. The mule follows the furrow straight along beneath his feet, crushing bones and flowers.

"Look," cried Nephthys, leaning out the window. Outside night falls in soundless clumps. "Do you hear the falcons that cry above golden fields? Do you see rats jumping over rocks ? Do you feel the silver cord hung about your neck? I am the sibyl, the sayer of secrets, voice of hidden things. I am blind until the moment I see through another soul's eyes. I am the cup of the lotus opening." She shines before me, sister of the dark, speaking dreams clothed in flesh. Nephthys, I turn round and round behind you. You are siren and friend and sorrower. We see what was never seen before. "I am light," she said. "I am the white, the infinite, the veil of brilliance. Give me your hand, brother, and we'll walk in spectral gardens. I shall lighten the valley."

Two candles dance upon the wick, filling the walls with shadow. I spin and dive through smoke. I repel the scorpion, the rat, the snake. I embrace the hair of your head. I come to raise order from chaos, to bind darkness with light. The shadows of history I smash to pieces. I change and change and change. I am the things left undone, words unsaid, hearts untouched, seeds unplanted. Look, at the shadow against the wall. It moves as you do. Its hands are yours. Clap them. Stamp your feet. Make your shadow dance. Is the dark all you have to fear?

Dreams. Dreams. All are dreams.

The east window fills with light. A thrush flies in and rests on the sill. Dew on his throat, songs on his throat, scarlet blood on his throat, he knows who he is. The sky has shaped his vision. He finds some nut or bug to eat, something to love, something to sing about.

The west window holds a dying flame. A swallow darts through shadows, catching moths, circling the orange glow of candles. Night rides in on her back. In her mouth lies the berry of god-thought, desire folded into her wings. She swoops, she dives in dark dreams, but perfect in darkness. The eye of a goddess opens and closes.

I stand before myself, a man of thoughts and bones and shadows. Before I was, I was the air I breathed today, the dirt I stood on; I was yesterday's sunset. Before I was born of woman, I lay curled in the egg of the world. I was dust, a fine powder of thought settling over the brown feet of women, the hooves of donkeys. I was the thought of myself sunning amid rocks and grasses. I greet myself on the right—that gentleman with a few hairs on his chest, the thought of his mother clinging in some far corner of his mind. To my left stands he who was his grandfather's song, who will be the aroma of his great granddaughter's bread. I am the world, a porous layer of skin, a drop of water, a reality. Out of the marshes I rose, the first flower of the papyrus. I am where I begin and end. When a fish leaps from water to water, in that moment of arc, he is a creature of air. So am I leaping from thought to thought, this life to that. So am I what I love.

I am a great, yellow, stalking cat—mesmerizer, healer, companion—tender and fierce, a beast of fur that blinks. I know what I know in my body. I hold the rat in my golden gaze. I lick the dust from my kittens. I am everywhere alert and at ease. I wait in the moment, no longer flesh and fur, but the fact of a thing that waits, patient and anonymous as stone. The air is my skin and cannot divide heaven from you, you from me, me from myself. We are two eyes aligned in a single vision. I am cat: pounce, paws and all. I am Mau, what I call myself. I am sun and dust, whiskers, milk and fur.

Bright, white Osiris stands, the perfume of lotus in a reflecting pool. He hovers about me, a question in search of answer. He bends his back to the plough, bends his head to the book, peers through the veil. I am his other one, the mover about of his bones, his fire. "Rise up," I shout. "There is work to do, fields to plow, mules to beat, goddesses to kiss. There are channels to fill with quick water, life to pour through the desert to make gardens bloom. There is air to breathe and I am the glad hairs of your nose. There are manure and sand to haul and long roads to walk where herbs sprout along the riverbank and lovers kiss unseen in the wind-carved cradle of rock. I'll take you where gazelles leap and lions follow in your shadow. I can show you the world in a kernel of wheat."

In the damp room waits a boy, dark-eyed, skin golden as sand, lips as red as pomegranate, eyebrows fine as a courtesan's. "I am Mestha, son of Horus, child of greening things," he said. "I am Mestha come to shake this house forever. I am the child becoming the man who will fill these rooms with grandchildren. I will raise corn and tell the young boys stories. I'll build houses and orchards and grape arbors. And when, as a bee, you come into my fields, I'll not chase you away, but smile and say: 'Look, children! Here flies your grandfather. Bless him, he always did love the vine.' I am Mestha, that which is the self, the personality, the soul of the man within the beast."

I enter the room where the ape child sits. Out of a sack he holds tumble blood and bones, viscera, arms and legs, backbones, hair and eyes—all the parts of a man, all my broken self. Out of chaos comes a life lived once, or perhaps only its possibility. The head rolls about the floor. Its eyes open, blink twice. Seeing himself in disarray, he pulls himself together by will or the mind, perhaps by love. He becomes himself, forms himself from the bits scattered around him. "I am Hapi, the thousand raindrops becoming river, the thousand days that make the memory. I recall a day when the sun shown full upon you—you were at the height of your powers—and you lifted me up, swinging, and carried me home to mother. You drove scorpions and snakes from the house at night. You built a house where every room opened onto sunrise. I am that child of your memory, and after you were gone, these thoughts lay with your bones. I recalled and reshaped you daily. You lived in me and I spoke your name in the memory of others and so we lived together day after day: a memory, a man, a name."

I come to the room where the sun rose. A hawk flies in and settles upon my wrist. In his mouth hangs the skin of a snake. "I am Horus," he cries. "From the land of kings I come, riding through the hot winds on the back of a jackal. Where priests murmured in crumbling temples, I flew through their sacred fires dropping feathers. In my beak I hold the poison. I bring nightmares to unbelievers. I come to shout the wisdom of air. I've come with a sycamore seed in my mouth. By the river we'll sow it and watch it grow through the years. You will die there, Osiris; and I will sit nine thousand years in the tree's white branches, one eye on each horizon, waiting for the return."

Through the last door of the house came a goose, waddling, a blue globe between his feet, pushing the blue egg of the world. "I am Geb-hassenef, your gosling son. Enter the egg and live in peace. On the day you were born, the world cracked open. When you die, the fissure heals itself. The egg rocks always back and forth. I've seen the flesh and bones of men, the sun coming and going in fire. In a moment the world changes as if by magic. I give you the anger and lust of the crocodile, and in the heat of love you shall transform them into will and desire. Your heart is a globe hanging in the east where the sun shines through. Your heart is an orb filling Egypt with amber light."

In the last room, in the center of the house grew the rod of heaven, a tree, a bone, a cock rising straight, quick as life. I come and go out the same door. I am the passage of time, the footfall of a hidden god, the prints of one already passed this way. I am what is left when the rest disappears. I stand a million years. I am the face in flowers, the mast of ships, the sails filling with gods' breath. From one land to another I carry you in myself. I am Osiris rising. No day passes that we are not part of each other. At dawn we hurry to the hills and wait for resurrection. To live and love and miss life when it's done, that is no disaster. We shall come home again.

A Field of Flowers

THE LOTUS GROWS QUIETLY IN the garden pool. The ibis curls one foot beneath him and blinks. It is too nice a day to spoil with words. In the wind I hear what I see—a low hum of vitality, the bell of flowers ringing. I pass in and out of time, eons press against my skin. I rest in a place within a place, a meadow of myself that is the world pressing close. The river flows on. Tall, thin reeds rock against the current, and the wind like a woman envelops me.

Life is liquid, cleansing, nourishing. I lie in the white mind of universe; knowing what I know, it knows me. The fruits of the land are abundant. With the quick, bright blade of spirit I turned new ground, planted seed. I struggled with the donkey. Beneath my hand things happened—grapes and wheat. In time I drank wine and ate bread. The field ploughed feeds a man, the spirit cultivated nourishes. I keep one eye on heaven and one on earth, following the seasons, walking the rhythm.

I lie on sweet hay. The sparrow's song cuts the silence. I hear it now as I heard it ages ago. The birds are gods. I carry their song in my belly. I'm carried in the egg of silence. Even now in the long pause of possibility, quiet beneath its shell, there rises a wild honking, long flights against an autumn moon, smooth eggs waiting to be laid. An old man lying in a field feels embryonic.

Learning peace itself is a struggle. More often I know the air as it whips my face. When the wind is still, I forget the wind. Walking through town, I turn longingly to the mountain. On the mountain I gaze back on the town. When there's much talk I withdraw into silence. When it is quiet I strain to hear some song. Having no trouble, I create some to keep the day interesting. We misunderstand the quiet. In the heat of the day I seek shadows. At night I praise the light of stars. The moon grows legs and wanders through an old man's heart seeking some dark corner to inspire. At midday the gods walk through town invisible as cats. Only children and wise old men know the difference.

Even night and day struggle, make peace between themselves. We call that beautiful sunset and dawn. In the spirits of men we call it a state of grace. Unless the earth enveloped the seed and the seed struggled against the darkness, there would be no corn. The moment we are born we begin to die. In each death we are born again. We take in the air and the air escapes us. Call it the breath of life. I no longer call loss disaster. It is the empty heart waiting to be filled. From the act of love, two bodies straining against each other, there rises the star of children. After opposition comes unity. Knowing that removes the sting of failure.

What god wants god shall have, and so I say, make it easy on yourself. The divine will asks only that things happen, that what it asks to exist comes to pass. My desire, my little will gives it form. If I struggle it comes anyway, malformed, a lesser power than it should be. If I give myself to it, it passes through me and I nourish it as it nourishes me. The difference is in the knowing of it. If there is confusion, I have not allowed life, the will of god, to change me. If I know it, I am changed by it. I have ferried myself across the churning waters of emotion. I go with the current; I rock to and fro in the tide. I come to a place I never knew I was bound for. There is a reason for accidents.

When I open my mouth I let the gods speak and it is like sparrows singing. When I open my heart I find the way, a gap through the wall of mountains. Through me I allow the world to unfold. I have the magic of earth, wind and flame. Though the future lies shrouded in veils, if I give my will to what I know not, I shall see it all come to pass. No sorrow. No sweat. Knowing the world is as the world should be, I enter the fields of peace.

Hymn to Ra

THE TRUTH OF WHAT WE call our knowing is both light and dark. Men are always dying and waking. The rhythm between we call life. In the night I turn and face myself, the many howling, laughing, pausing in the body of one. Some miracle is about to happen. Some new man unseen wishes to rise and speak. I walk in the dark feeling darkness on my skin. Dawn always begins in the bones. The light stirs me to rise and walk. Lightly I step around the sleeping forms, the bodies of the other selves still dreaming. Nothing has been disturbed except my inner quiet. I am restless, an animal sniffing the wind. The shape of truth is coming.

Death matters, as does life. As it ends it begins again. Knowing that is both my comfort and fear. Perfection is a long road; I shall never see its end—the ribbon of life winds back on itself. At dawn the threads of time unfurl, sunlight streams across the sands. Time reaches in both directions, knotted in the golden orb of the moment. The eye opens, the heart opens, the navel yawns and takes the world in its belly. Beneath him the snake feels the movement of earth. Everything else is sky. This moment is eternity.

This light I call genius, noble being conversant with gods. He goes out, hears the hum of the world, beings of light muttering in every stream. In every rock and tree he hears god songs. Then he returns and tells me what god said. I flow like blood from the god's wounds. I am the god's life made visible. I am how god comes to know himself, his ears, his hands, his eyes. The dreaming selves stir in the dark and follow the distant song of the lyre. We enter grace and beauty. I am Osiris shining.

And at dawn I leave my house and go into the field. Stars fade like memory. Bless the boat of morning that carries us into light. Bless the oars that stir the water causing ripples of consciousness. Bless the northern and southern edges of sky. Bless the eastern and western banks of the river. Bless the oarsmen in the boat, god's people, his faith, his creation. Bless the face of god above us and the reflection of god on earth below. Bless the veil of clouds that guard his secrets. Bless life stirring below the surface of skin, the discomfort of human weakness and mortality, loss and suffering, the misunderstandings that prick consciousness and prod men toward truth. Bless the goddesses, the wives, the daughters, the mothers, the priestesses. Bless the house of Osiris. Bless this body where the world is gathered. Bless the light in his forehead, in his heart and hands. Bless the sun that shines on every limb.

A creature of light am I.

Hymn to Osiris

THE DOORS OF PERCEPTION OPEN; what was hidden has been revealed. It is myself I see and a thousand colors swirling in liquid light. I am where the sun sets below the mountains. I am in this body. I am that star rising above clouds hung by a thread from its ocean moon. Hail myself traversing eternity walking among gods, a shuttle flying across the loom through the threads of time. This is all one place, one cloth: a man's life endures. On earth flowers grow, snakes crawl and wisdom lies in the palm of a hand. All that is will be—hawks and sparrows, the thousand lives within.

I have come home. I have entered humanhood, bound to rocks and plants, men and women, rivers and sky. I shall be with you in this and other worlds. When the cat arches in the doorway, think of me. I have sometimes been like that. When two men greet each other in the street, I am there speaking to you. When you look up, know I am there—sun and moon pouring my love around you. All these things am I, portents, images, signs. Though apart, I am a part of you. One of the million things in the universe, I am the universe, too. You think I disguise myself as rivers and trees simply to confuse you? Whatever I am, woman, cat or lotus, the same god breathes in every body. You and I together are a single creation. Neither death nor spite nor fear nor ignorance stops my love for you.

May we come and go in and out of heaven through the gates of starlight. As the houses of earth fill with dancing and song, so filled are the houses of heaven. I come, in truth. I sail a long river and row back again. It is joy to breathe under the stars. I am the sojourner destined to walk a thousand years until I arrive at myself.

Hymn to Hathor

BLUE-LIDDED DAUGHTER OF DAWN, golden lady of the mountains, carrier of her father's wisdom, let an old man rest in your arms. Let him look last on love's face, breathing love's breath. I live in light a million years. The sun rises or sets now—it matters not. Here is ecstasy in death and certainty in life. We are gods in the body of god, truth and love our destinies. Go then and make of the world something beautiful, set up a light in the darkness.

Appendix

A Few Ways to Use *Awakening Osiris* for Spiritual Writing Practice

The ancient scribes worked on writing and copying the Books of the Afterlife for their clients, who were illiterate but had very spiritual beliefs and needs. Like these ancient priest scribes, I will show you ways of using *Awakening Osiris* as a template for creating your own Book of Coming into Light.

The most important thing to remember before we begin is that the ancient Egyptians believed that words were magical (*heka*), and that beautiful, well-crafted prayers (*medju neter*) were efficacious. As you work with the ideas in this appendix, work them with specific intention and attention to details. God and gods are in the details. As Meister Eckhart said: "Apprehend God in all things for God is in all things. Every creature is filled with God and is a book about God."

Chapter Table of Contents to Your Book of the Dead

Every ancient scribe knew the full title to their own copy of the Book of the Afterlife. It recounted the chapters and the purposes of their inscriptions. Writing the title page for your own personal Book of the Dead (interchangeable with Book of the Afterlife and Book of Coming Forth into Light) usually occurs at the *end*, after you have finished writing the text, but the title page, of course, is placed at the beginning.

Feel free to use your own chapter titles, object names, and metaphors mixed and matched with the ancient language of spells and magic. Be specific. Be metaphoric. Be humble. Be bold. Be radiant and unafraid.

Remember, it can be revised as your life changes. Oh, yes, and your life can be revised. That is the point, after all.

Here is an ancient Egyptian title for the Book of the Dead:

The Book of Coming Forth by Day
And the Book of What Is in Duat
In order to know the ba souls of Duat, to know what is done, to know the
    spiritual enlightenment of Re,
To know the secret ba souls,
To know what happens in the hours of the night and their gods,
To know the gates and the ways in which the great gods pass,
To know the flourishing and the annihilated.

Here is my version thereof:

Inscribed in the House of Life
The book of repelling the crocodile—called avarice, envy, greed.
Protection for the heart in every hour, the carriage of the vessel.
The book of coming forth by day; the book of coming into night.
Protection of the family, the community, the earth.
The book of appeasing the desires of Sekhmet.
The inventory of the mind and heart.
The alchemical processes in the astral and physical.
Knowing the offerings of myrrh, pomegranate, breath, and beer.
Knowing the secret forms of the goddess and the god.
Their divinity having been laid bare and yet cloaked in invisibility.
The writing of daily transformations, poems of the day, every day
so that these divine souls remain in place
Never to leave this sacred temple—ever—
The book of magical protection.
A list of all the sacred places, known and untouched.
The eternal return of two heavenly bodies.
O Seshet, my soul is an open scroll.

Say My Name That I May Live

When I walk through graveyards, whether modern or ancient ones, I repeat the names of the deceased that appear on their stones, and I pray

"May he/she rest in peace." The tombs of the Egyptians have offering inscriptions, called *hotep*. These carved ritual hieroglyphs depict an offering table with bread, wine or beer, and/or other foods upon a table covered by a ritual cloth. This was the original "Holy Communion" with the dead that became a Samhain ritual, a ritual for the Day of the Dead, or the Catholic sacrament. Hotep is the word for "peace." When it appeared in tombs or on gravestones, it meant "Rest in Peace." Beautiful chapters of offerings appear carved upon the door lintels, door stoops, and around the door frames.

The naming of the dead offers a kind of obituary, recounting that person's many names. (Often, we are known by many names.) These inscriptions tell the stories of ancestors, of the places we lived, by whom we were loved, their titles, and the deeds enacted for the benefit of the community, and so on.

This powerful ritual aligns the soul and the god spark of the deceased individual with the Light of the Creator. The Litany of Ra proclaims, "I am entirely a god. No limb of mine is without God. I enter as a God. I exit as a God. The Gods have transformed themselves into my body. . . . God is my name. I do not forget this name of mine."

Say My Name that I May Live is a prayer that may be spoken for the birth of a child into this world, or as a prayer for deliverance at the end of a life. Many memorials use this prayer technique. I have seen it used to remember the dead and the ancestors as we visited the Great Pyramid, and I used the "Knot of Isis" as a part of this naming ritual when I distributed my mother's ashes in Philae.

When the 9/11 tragedy happened, my dear friend Reverend Laura Janesdaughter of the Temple of Isis in Los Angeles contacted me asking permission to use the work in *Awakening Osiris* in honor of the dead. We received the names of a group of individuals who died on those fatal flights. For the next seventy-two days, daily prayers and ritual mourning were performed to honor those spirits, as the ancients might have done.

Yes, I wrote *Awakening Osiris*, but the late Laura Janesdaughter made this ritual a beautiful ceremony. Here is information about that ceremony. I gave her permission to use my work, and now I ask her posthumously to grant me permission to reprint her ceremony. This record of her work appeared online and is hosted by the Fellowship of Isis.

Ritual and Prayer for Victims of September 11th

On Thursday, September 20, 2001, at 6:38 pm, Laura Janesdaughter of Temple of Isis Los Angeles sent out the following message:

A Call to Nebhet Work: The Goddess of Transitional Death

Dear Friends,

It was my 60th birthday on Monday and as part of my birthday work, I find that I have been called to organize an effort to Name the people who died in the terrorist attacks last week in New York City, Pennsylvania, and Washington, DC, and offer prayers to them in the name of Nebhet/ Nephthys and Her Dark Sisters to help them through their transitions.

Somehow the Naming is important and though I'm sure all will be Named somewhere else, few will focus on this aspect. It also seems important that the work be done between now and Samhain.

This work can be whatever you might wish it to be, and I have some suggestions inspired by some things other people have done should you wish them.

This seems like a daunting task but can be done. Please email me if you (or a group you represent) would like to participate. I'm not quite sure yet how to go about "organizing" who has been Named by whom but will figure this out soon.

Meanwhile, if you have someone or ones you'd like to undertake, please let me know.

May the Wings of Nebhet protect and guide those who perished,

Laura Janesdaughter

"To live is to die a thousand deaths, but there is only one fire, one eternity."

—BECOMING THE PHOENIX FROM *AWAKENING OSIRIS*,
translated by Normandi Ellis

While the initial networking with those interested in participating in this important work began, Laura and her group members obtained lists of the names of those who had been killed on September 11. This included those who had died in the bombings, those who had died in the crashed airplanes, and those rescue workers who had lost their lives.

The names were divided and distributed among thirty volunteers, and the work began. We were called upon to say prayers daily for the deceased, mentioning their names one at a time, with the petition "Say my name that I may live." This work continued for seventy days without ceasing, in accordance with ancient Egyptian tradition.

Each participant performed the same basic observances, but each was free to add on to this simple rite whatever devotions seemed personally appropriate. The usual method of working was to light a candle on the altar as each name was spoken aloud, say the prayer "Say my name that I may live," and then strike a chime or bell.

FOI members from the United States, Australia, Germany, Canada, and the United Kingdom participated in this seventy-day ritual of Naming the Dead (*https://www.foicentral.org*).

Laura Janesdaughter, the editor of *The Isis Papers*, wrote in the editorial of this issue:

> *I had felt called to make some commitment because of my birthday and then I knew—in the Name of Nebhet, Goddess of Transitional Death, the Names of the Dead could be Named. It took me a week to work up to asking other people to participate in the Naming. When I sent the first message out, Normandi Ellis immediately responded and said that "Say my name that I may live" was an ancient petition and so this became the common prayer that 30 women who participated have used for Naming. We have Named 2,000 of the September 11th Dead so far. At the FOI Convocation at Isis Oasis, the TOI/LA women and others lit 343 candles on the steps of the Temple for the New York Fire Department men who died and spoke all of their Names. I went out around 1 am on Sunday morning to see this blazing Altar of flames and souls united— and felt I had done Her Work and was now Her Priestess.*

Those of us who participated in this work with Laura and TOI/LA and attended the Convocation at Isis Oasis in 2001 will never forget the sight of those candles glowing on the steps outside the Isis Chapel at Isis Oasis Sanctuary. The Naming of the Dead was a profound and important work, which sprang into being through the conscience and loving heart of a devoted Priestess.

Chapters to be used during the ritual were: "Becoming the Phoenix," "The Knot of Isis," and "Remembering His Name."

How to Write Your Own "Say My Name" Prayer (from Invoking the Scribes)

We often make subtle shifts over time. The following exercise reminds us of what matters and where we are in our path of life's unfolding. This writing is a sacred remembrance and self-discovery; it may be composed once in a lifetime or as often as once a year. Many of my naming poems were written with schoolchildren who were studying Walt Whitman's "Song of Myself," one of the great naming poems of all time. Feel free to adapt this model to your own needs.

In general, the naming poem will have the following components:

- greeting the divine
- naming yourself, your current name, and all the names you've ever had—pet names, family names, married names, sacred names
- listing memories that arise as those names are spoken
- naming ancestors, parents, grandparents, important persons or places
- naming activities that represent your essential self at this time
- naming those you love, those whose lives have intersected with your own
- naming places you've lived or held sacred
- describing how you have heard the voice of God or served the divine. What in that Spirit moves you?
- aligning yourself with the divine presence
- naming yourself again

- stating a feeling to conclude the prayer, such as "I am . . . [feeling]" and why you feel that way

As an example, I include this naming poem written by Cathleen Shattuck in 2009 during a class I taught as we sailed down the Nile in Egypt. It appeared in the book *Invoking the Scribes* and is used here with permission.

I Am the Name

Say my name that I may live, Cathleen
from Waterville, Vermont, high up on a
winding dirt road that ended at my uncle's home.
Twiss Hill, one of many roads named for
farmsteads broken up over the years.
I have two sets of relatives. Those that
are dead, and those that are adopted
never intended to count. She was adopted.
He was adopted. "They aren't really family."
I dream my Irish mother rode in
on an Orphan Train.

Say my name so that I may live, Cathleen.
My grandmother worked for
Rolls Royce in England, read tea leaves in America.
My great, great grandmother divorced
her husband, set up shop on her own
in New York, Connecticut.
The men—sailors, or tobacconists,
Green Mountain Boys, fighters, farmers.

Say my name, Cathleen,
Daughter of a navy man
and a teacher, before we moved again
and they began
again in retirement to caretake
the cemetery, the roses, the names scattered
about, some of them the same as mine.
Peaceful Mountain View.

Say my name, Cathleen,
who at age twelve once taught Bible School
before revulsion at the robotic
resuscitation of Bible verses
by toddlers turned my head
permanently from the land-greedy
people of the Nazarene.

Say my name, Cathleen.
I love fiddlehead ferns and the taste
of cattail roots pulled white and gleaming
from the mud, sucking the frail
vials of nectar from the clover,
legs scratched by accidentally haying
while wear shorts. My mother makes me
French toast before school
if I ask her. There is a pitcher of maple
sap, not syrup, sap, in the fridge
just tapped from the tree.
It tastes like a cold, sweet snowstorm.
The chickadee changes its song.

If your tough, you're
"wicked rugged"; if it's just cool
its "wicked" b'Jesus.
Canada is just over the border,
eh? On a hot day it's time
to swim in the river. Avoid
slow moving water for there'll
be leaches.

Say my name, Cathleen.
My yard is a hayfield, the bobolinks
dancing on the edges of the grass. My yard is
a cornfield when the farmer who rents our
land decides to change the seed.
My yard is the cemetery where I spend
endless hours helping my parents.

I am an expert at moving fake flowers
and digging moss away from the plot
markers, initialized like so many
monogrammed cuff links.
The smell of cow manure
is unavoidable, saddle leather,
the must of the hay barn,
the pop of tractor exhaust,
flowers, donuts being
made in the kitchen.

Say my name, Cathleen,
reared in the ways of Anubis
hovering over the tended grave,
playing with the ghosts
who live in the caved-in plots
that we gently fill with sod,
flaking the lichen from stone.

Hymns to the Divine—Using the Personal Universe

Hymns and prayers to the divine come in two forms. One of them is the simple poem of praise, adoration, or supplication, such as the chapters called "Greeting Ra" and the "Hymn to Hathor." The other is an aretalogy, a poetic immersion in the life of the divine one, spoken in the first person; the author assumes the divine nature of the deity and speaks, such as the chapter called "Awakening Osiris."

There was not one simple prayer to one god in any one Book of the Dead; there are many collected aretalogies, prayers, and hymns that could be addressed to many gods and goddesses. The multiple versions of hymns to the same god or goddess appear in the collection like bouquets of flowers upon an altar. In the Papyrus of Ani's Book, hymns to Osiris and Ra often appeared together as a sign of the soul's capacity to live and die and become resurrected multiple times. Likened to the rising and setting sun, these pastoral prayers are imbued with specific language—the more specific, the better. They demonstrate a joyous celebration of life and often expounded on the glory of daily activities.

I think of these poets and scribes as everyday shamans of the human experience. The beautifully particular words were the magic that captured that place and time. Shamans often carry around their necks a pouch of colored stones, tobacco, feathers, plant medicine—all with powers to heal, to banish, to invoke, and to praise. While I worked on the hymns, I carried the language of poetry around my throat—the specificity of star, pomegranate seed, hawk, malachite, and so on. These were the words that I used to invoke the heart of Egypt. I meditated on the individual hieroglyphs of the hymns to a particular deity and then explored the particularities of their imagery. I vocalized their onomatopoeia, the sibilant language that reminded me of their names. I gleaned their stories from ancient texts, but more importantly, I explored how my story linked to theirs. What attributes and legends had called me to become their priestess scribe?

One of the things that you can do is to explore the sanctity of your own sacred language—the words, the images, the fullness of the vowels, and the shapes of the sounds in your throat. To do that, let us make a list on slips of paper of one hundred words. Nothing too abstract, these are words that thrill our hearts, our minds, and our mouths. Let us think in particularities: I would ask you to create one hundred words that bring into your life love, joy, and emotional resonance with the world:

- 16 words that are specific images (like smoke, toad, willow, cloud, etc.)
- 16 words that are specific sounds (like thunder, trickle, roar, whisper, etc.)
- 16 words that are specific smells (like baby, myrrh, rain, grass, etc.)
- 16 words that are specific tastes—often linked to smells (like salt, coffee, vinegar, tangerine, etc.)

- 16 words that are specific tactile feelings, which means something you can feel on your body or with your fingers (like skin, sand, silk, wind, etc.)
- 10 words that are specific movements (like slap, ride, dance, sleep, etc.)
- 10 favorite words that include 3 abstractions, such as wisdom; peace; a day of the week; a part of the body; a number, an animal, a familial relationship, and so on

Remember, some words do double or triple duty. For example, smoke is an action, it is a smell, and it is an image; tangerine is a taste, and a color, and an image.

Put these words in a jar where you can access them while you are writing. Because we write and read in English, it takes some symbolism and poetic effort to bring the spark back into the hymns of the particular world in the ways that Walt Whitman, Mary Oliver, Pablo Neruda, and Nagib Mafouz are wont to do.

You can use these words in repeating patterns that become a one-word refrain, as "My heart, my mother; my heart, my mother; my heart of my becoming." Or a refrain of petition as in "Triumph through the Cities," where we explore diverse aspects of Thoth. Each paragraph begins, "Hail, Thoth, architect of truth . . . !" and is followed by a supplication. Remember the words are not the poem. You are the poem, and the words are a spontaneous creative imagery that reflects the personal self. The hieroglyphs were the Egyptians' alchemy of transformation. The personal universe is our equivalent process.

Writing Aretalogies

As mentioned above, aretalogies are poetic embodiments of the power of the god or goddess. *Awakening Osiris* is filled with phrases that double as moments of transformation into the divinity itself. Simply put, the incantation begins and is knitted throughout with the use of the words "I am." When you write an aretalogy, you become a vessel for that deity's energy; you allow its story and language to pass through you. Or the piece can become an oracular trance, a prognostication, or an epic tale, as in "Giving Breath to Osiris."

Because the Book of the Dead is all about the dissolution of mortal consciousness and the acquisition of supraconsciousness, the true divine spark, it turns itself into a metaphor for becoming this or that divine being. Inert flesh and bone become light in the way Osiris becomes Ra. All of *Awakening Osiris* is how that is done.

One way to dedicate oneself to a goddess or god in life is by engaging in writing such aretalogies. In my book *Dreams of Isis*, I took on the form and the story of Isis, based on a healing hymn to Isis written in gratitude by a shipwrecked sailor whom she healed. I might add that at that time in my life, I, too, was a shipwrecked sailor. That poem is a rather long, straightforward aretalogy called "Hymn of Isis," in which recognized what I had lost and the power I still had during that dark night of the soul. I clung to her skirt and pulled it over me; Isis pulled me through it.

Whether an aretalogy is long or short, the power of writing it is that it becomes healing medicine. In this book, "The Knot of Isis" is a shorter hymn in which the writer claims the goddess power of the amulet of fertility and renewal called the *thet*.

> *I am the knot where two worlds meet. Red magic courses through my veins like the blood of Isis, magic of Magic, spirit of Spirit. I am proof of the power of the goddess. I am water and dust walking.*

Creating Amulets and Words of Power

The natural world is the "godded" world and is filled with divine magic. Seeds sprout into wheat; rivers flood and the soil is replenished. The ancient Egyptians kept an eye on the cycles of time and the renewals brought about by the patterns of change—life and death and transformation. Every living thing had consciousness, an inner knowing of what was necessary to attain its divine inheritance. This becoming was the true mystery of the Black Land of Egypt, which was called al-Khemy. (Khem was the name for Egypt.) It was the power of conscious becoming that turns death into life. And of one thing the priest sorcerers were certain: There is no end of becoming.

The scarab beetle was the image par excellence of transformation of death into life, darkness into light. Behind the naos in the sanctuary of Edfu, one finds a winged beetle carved on the wall at the level of the heart. That beetle is the key to mutable states of consciousness. "In the beginning I came into being. I have become the becoming," says Khepera in "The History of Creation." "I came into being as I came into being. I grew as I grew. I changed as I change."

The power of transformation is wrapped inside the mummy, wound into the binding cloths. Amulets of transformation cover the wounds of the body and protect the soul from falling into ennui. What are these amulets? Eyes of Horus, Thets, Ankhs, the Heart, the Winged Scarab, and images of the various deities—jackal, hawk, ibis, and so on. Ancient Egyptians loved the idea of potentiality. And so, there were chapters of "Becoming the Falcon of Gold," "Becoming the Crocodile," "Becoming the Phoenix," and so on.

To write a Becoming Hymn, you may choose a hieroglyph that appeals or choose one of the words from your personal universe. Hold that word close to your heart and consciousness. Fall into its story, feel the air that moves around it, the colors of the sky, stone, and even its own body. What lesson can that particular being teach? Begin with the words of becoming: "I Am" and feel your way into the poem. What are its qualities? What does this neter (the consciousness of the god or goddess) want? What does it dream? What has it overcome? What does it know? Read "Becoming the Swallow" to see how the becoming poems can be written as trancelike oracles of potentiality and wisdom.

Mapping the Journey and Hours of the Night

Negotiating the halls of the underworld became the most important reason for the many different versions of the books of the afterlife. As the soul followed the path of the sun into the duat and emerged again at morning, it entered twelve halls, or hours of night. These were places that existed inside the body of the sky goddess Nut, mother of all, who birthed and consumed the energy of the souls back into their origin. Within her body were spirit beings—guardians, messengers, and heralds—who had to be acknowledged and whose names must be known.

All souls pass through these chambers as part of their transformation and ascension into light beings. One might also find these places and people as part of a dreamscape. For the living, these halls represent "dark nights of the soul" through which we must travel. It is good to know one's shadow and greet it, in order to pass through a difficult time. It is good to know the map of the under (or inner) world while we live. Thus, it was said that the scribe who wrote the book of the dead over and over throughout her lifetime was a thousand times blessed.

In the tomb of Seti I there is a very long title that explains what is contained in the text.

Treatise of the Hidden Chamber,
To know the positions of the Ba-souls, the gods, the shadows, the
    Akh-spirits,
and what is done.
The beginning is the horn of the West, the gate of the western horizon,
the end is thick darkness, the gate of the western horizon.
To know the Ba-souls of the Duat,
to know what is done, to know their spiritualization for Re, to know the
    secret Ba-souls,
to know what is in the hours and their gods, to know what he calls to them,
to know the gates and the ways upon which the great god passes,
to know the courses of the hours and their gods,
to know the flourishing and the annihilated.

In *Awakening Osiris,* a number of chapters with similar content became part of the afterlife document. These various versions probably represented the possible texts available for purchase by an individual and inserted into his text. Ani, because he was the master teacher of scribes, had access to these many different texts; therefore, all of those versions of variant texts became a part of his. Negotiating passage through the underworld and knowing who one might meet was required. For example, the chapter of *Awakening Osiris* called "Twenty-One Women" depicted the soul riding through the underworld on the back of a serpent. The text and imagery resonate with the art found in the tomb of Tutmosis III in the Valley of the Kings in which the coffin slides down into the various levels and halls of the underworld, being moved along on the back of a serpent.

Another chapter of the beings in duat is "Seven Houses in the Other World." In this chapter, one greets the various shadows of the self and speaks their names. Other books of the dead have the soul address the shadows and guardians with the phrase, "I know you. I know your name." As I mentioned before, these guardians are shadow images of an inner landscape. Three beings (a guardian, a herald, and a messenger) each attend seven doors. They are some of the seventy-two shadows of Ra, which are the unconscious or subconscious attributes that must be acknowledged in order to grow in light.

"Triumph Over Darkness" would be an introduction to these duat beings. That chapter reminds us that "the ways of light are numerous."

As a writing practice, try crafting a poem similar to the two chapters "Twenty-One Women" or "Seven Houses in the Other World."

- What have been your challenges in this life? You may choose to greet them by decade, looking back on the passages you made through your youth, adult life, middle age, etc.
- Can you name the moment you left behind your innocence (herald)? What happened?

- Who gave you the wisdom that allowed you to pass through this experience (guardian)?
- What lesson did you glean from the event (messenger)?
  Try to see these events not simply as challenges, but as gifts from the universe. That is the purpose of karma—the teaching. Every day and in every situation, we learn how to turn death consciousness into life consciousness.
- End each recognition with a blessing, such as "Blessed is the lady."

The Negative Confession

The judgment scenes in the Halls of Ma'at wherein one stands before the Lord of the underworld show the culmination of patterns we have lived. Truth is written upon our heart, which is weighed in the balance against the feather of Ma'at. To pass into the spirit world, one's heart must weigh as light as a feather. Our lies and sins, both unconscious and conscious errors, have been inscribed upon the heart. The negative confession is a cultural statement of personal ethics. The idea is to approach the judgment day with one's heart as light as a feather.

With time and committed work, we can gain true wisdom. In life, we can ask forgiveness, own up to our darkness, name our shadows, and make amends. Khepera assures us that change is not only possible but also something to be desired. Sin is a thought that misses the mark; therefore, change the thought while you live and live the renewed understanding of universal love for one's family, neighbor, community, one's god, and oneself.

Whether or not you or a family member is an alcoholic, the practices and the twelve steps inside the Big Book of Alcoholics Anonymous can, if followed, make sweeping changes in your life. By recognizing a higher power and taking an in-depth moral inventory of ourselves—then making amends to those we have harmed—we can gain enlightenment. Enlightenment is the whole point of making one's heart as light as a feather.

The negative confession of the Egyptians is similar in practice to the AA inventory. Statements include such things as "I have not caused anyone to weep," or "I have not stolen food," or "I have not been an eavesdropper." There are forty-two so-called Negative Confessions, some of which are comparable to the Ten Commandments, such as "I have not committed adultery," "I have not blasphemed the gods," and so on. Every spiritual tradition has a similar code of ethics. The Negative Confessions are not a list of prohibitions, nor are they a denial, as some believe them to be. They are an affirmation of ways and means of right conduct for living with others. Remember that the world responds to our thoughts, and our thoughts and actions create our reality. Ma'at rules the foundation of all creation and creative thought—the laws of karma and reciprocity, balance, growth, and the law of love, as well as the law of mind.

Awakening Osiris has two sections that relate to the forty-two Negative Confessions; they are "Entering Truth" and "The Confessions." Remember, writing affirmations and negative confessions can be a way of changing one's life story so that you change your way of thinking and being. Remember that everything you do in your life can be and should be done as a co-creator with Spirit. The truth of Ma'at exists in physical, astral, mental, and spiritual planes, and all these thoughts and actions exist in the akashic record, which may be another way of thinking of the heart balanced against the scale of Ma'at. One must keep a watchful eye on one's processes and energies. It is good to periodically reread the Budge version of the forty-two confessions of Ani, then to craft your own confessions based on that.

Make a covenant with Ma'at to be ever vigilant and mindful. You cannot fudge or walk in the gray areas when dealing with Ma'at. Silence is preferable to even a slight alteration of truth. Here is a practice from *The Union of Isis and Thoth* that may enhance your work with Ma'at.

In meditation, immerse yourself in a cleansing bath of stars. Step into the awesome spaciousness of the firmament and find the presence of the goddess Ma'at who wears the white ostrich feather upon her head. Ask her to strip away any veils you may have over your eyes. Ask her to show you any errors in your thinking or your actions. Ask for complete knowledge of yourself. Pay careful attention to her answers. You cannot be true to another unless you are in truth with yourself. Look deeply into the eyes of Ma'at, knowing that she stands before you as the representative of all the divine beings, all humanity, and of your own deepest self. Her eyes are the sparkling color of clear liquid pools of night sky, and when you know that she sees you, put your hand upon your heart and say:

"I vow to you: conscious speech, compassionate action, and purity of heart."

Say this three times. Ask for wisdom and a blessing.

Now, you may write your negative confession of forty-two things that represent your spiritual code of ethics at this time of your life.

Healing and the Bodies of Light

Dreams of Isis offers a teaching on the nine bodies of the ancient Egyptians and how all of these bodies operate on the astral, mental, and spiritual levels. All nine are living bodies wrapped in the cocoon of physical flesh. Healing our physical, mental, astral, and spiritual bodies allows us to become a temple of light. That is the ascension practice. Although you can find much more in my book *Dreams of Isis*, I offer this delineation in brief.

In the spiritual realm, we find the god spark, our initiating principle akh; the soul, ba; and the animating spirit, ka. In the mental realm, we find the body called ren that names our experiences; the sekhem, our will; and the ib or ab, which we have already identified as the heart, or seat of consciousness. In the astral realm appear the light body, sahu; the shadow or ghost known as khaibit; and the aufu, or astral body.

All of these are enclosed inside the living khat, the mortal coil. At death they unravel and release, but while we live, they live in us. Thus, one may experience a number of altered states while living with them. We carry them with us throughout our lives. We carry their stories wrapped around us like mummy rags when we cross, unless we learn to release them while we live. Spiritual journal writing helps with that release.

Some of the most important chapters in *Awakening Osiris* are those chapters that petition the god to be granted a mouth, to untie the rags from one's face. It does one no good to be tongue-tied before the gods during judgement. Imagine trying to hold all your secrets inside while you are living, then suddenly, at death, the string of words unspoken bind you. Confession, it is said, is good for the soul. No one has to read this but you. Having met Ma'at and been given truth, ask for the "words of power," the heka that is the magic spell of release. Ask to remember your true name, the names of the ancestors, the places you lived, all those memories that are part of your true story that become the key to your true destiny. As the ancient spells said, "Say my name that I may live."

Write your naming poem following the instructions on page 182. One of the most blessed, glorious poems of naming oneself comes from Walt Whitman's poem "Song of Myself." In it, he goes beyond the boundaries of his personal story and becomes the story of his country, of the environment, of the universe itself. The poem is bounding and glorious. As the Egyptians would have said in similar celebration, "God is my name. I do not forget this name of mine"; try ending your writing by saying the same thing.

Among the other healing hymns of the spiritual bodies is the healing of the heart, especially when life experiences tear us asunder. The chapter "Not Letting His Heart Be Carried Off" recognizes that transformation derives from our desire nature and that change can be made through application of will. Other chapters of self-preservation are "Not Scattering His Bones," "Not Dying a Second Time," "Not Losing His Mind," and "Not Decaying in the Other World." These were possible scenarios that derive from abuse of a corpse. Such is the case in the ancient world, when one is buried with many jewels and gold.

But you may want to write your healing and protection hymns to protect yourself while you live. Write a healing poem akin to "Not Losing His Mind" when your heart is broken, your ego is hurt, or you wish to compose one for an elder who suffers from dementia and needs you to assist in memory. If you say her name, she can live. It is a beautiful thing to do for another person.

Healing amulets found their ways between the winding sheets of the mummy; thus were the prayers for the dead taken with them. These amulets included the red carnelian thet (or Knot of Isis), the green winged scarab, the blue or carnelian heart, the blue lapis lazuli and malachite Eye of Horus, and so on. A hymn was recited over these objects to activate their protective powers, and the amulets were anointed with oils. The hymns were taken with the deceased in the underworld, but the amulets were wrapped up in the body rags.

The Gratitudes and Be-Attitudes

Our lives are filled with lists—to-do lists, grocery lists, honey-do lists, roll calls, and appointments. Forget it and instead keep a gratitude journal. This is the most important list of all. It only takes a few minutes to record five beautiful things a day for which you are grateful: white cumulus cloud like a roaring lion on a blue sky, club cracker with pimento cheese, an afternoon nap, a deep red unfurling dahlia, natural blond streaks in my daughter's dark brown hair.

If you record five things every day, you will have 1,825 beautiful things in a year—something beautiful for every season. Stay awake. Try not to repeat anything. Find more than five things every day. Find beauty in things that did not seem beautiful at the time. Be grateful that spirit watches over us, keeps us out of harm's way, and teaches us patience. Slow down. Pay attention.

When I am on the dahabeya floating along the Nile in Egypt, I rest my eyes on the beautiful people and things that I had only imagined seeing forty years ago. "I have known the charms of old sycamore trees, children hanging apelike from sturdy branches, or passing clouds snatched for a moment by green leaves, or cattle lowing in the shade. And I know the lifeless sand that forms after the tree is gone. To the trees I make offerings of water. In this way I paid homage to gods."

With an attitude of gratitude, I create continuing abundance.

Bibliography

Breasted, James H. *The Dawn of Conscience*. New York: Charles Scribner's Sons, 1933.

———. *A History of Egypt*. New York: Charles Scribner's Sons, 1948.

———. *Ancient Records of Egypt: Historical Documents from the Earliest Times to the Persian Conquest*. 5 vols. New York: Russell & Russell, 1962.

———. *Egyptian Servant Statues*. (Bollingen series, no. 13.) New York: Pantheon Books, 1948.

Budge, E. A. Wallis. *The Book of the Dead: The Hieroglyphic Transcript of the Papyrus of Ani*. Secaucus, NJ: University Books, 1960.

———. *The Dwellers on the Nile*. New York: Dover, 1977.

———. *The Egyptian Book of the Dead* (The Papyrus of Ani). New York: Dover, 1967.

———. *Egyptian Magic*. New York: Dover, 1971.

———. *The Gods of the Egyptians*. 2 vols. New York: Dover, 1969.

Casson, Lionel. *Daily Life in Ancient Egypt*. New York: American Heritage Publishing, 1975.

Davenport, Guy (trans.) *Maxims of the Ancient Egyptians*. Louisville, KY: Pace Trust Co., 1981.

Eliade, Mircea. *A History of Religious Ideas*, vol. 1. Chicago: University of Chicago Press, 1978.

Erman, Adolf. *Life in Ancient Egypt*. New York: Dover, 1971.

Frazer, J. G. *Adonis, Attis, Osiris*. London: Macmillan, 1906.

Frankfort, Henri. *Ancient Egyptian Religion*. New York: Harper & Row, 1948.

Gardiner, Sir Alan. *Egypt of the Pharaohs*. London: Oxford University Press, 1961.

———. *Egyptian Grammar*, 3rd ed. Oxford: Griffith Institute, 1957.

Golding, William. *An Egyptian Journal*. New York: Faber & Faber, 1986.

Greener, Leslie. *The Discovery of Egypt*. New York: Viking, 1967.

Griffith, F. L., and Herbert Thompson. *The Leyden Papyrus. An Egyptian Magical Book*. New York: Dover, 1979.

Herodotus. *The Histories*. Trans. by Aubrey de Selincourt. Harmondworth: Penguin Classics, 1954.

Hussein, Mohamed A. *Origins of the Book: From Papyrus to Codex*. Greenwich, CT: New York Graphic Society, 1972.

Ions, Veronica. *Egyptian Mythology*. New York: Peter Bedrick Books, 1968.

Lamy, Lucie. *Egyptian Mysteries: New Light on Ancient Spiritual Knowledge*. New York: Crossroad Publishing, 1981.

Lesko, Leonard H. *The Ancient Egyptian Book of Two Ways*. Berkeley: University of California Press, 1972.

Lichtheim, Miriam. *Ancient Egyptian Literature*. 2 vols. Berkeley: University of California Press, 1973.

Lurker, Manfred. *The Gods and Symbols of Ancient Egypt*. London: Thames and Hudson, 1980.

Mertz, Barbara. *Temples, Tombs and Hieroglyphs*. New York: Dell, 1964.

Plutarch. "Isis and Osiris," in vol. V of the *Moralia*, ed & trans. by F. C. Babbitt. London: Loeb Classical Library, 1936.

Pope, Maurice. *The Story of Archaeological Decipherment: From Egyptian Hieroglyphs to Linear B*. New York: Charles Scribner's Sons, 1975.

Pound, Ezra, and Noel Stock. *Love Poems of Ancient Egypt*. New York: New Directions, 1962.

Pritchard, J. B. (ed.). *Ancient Near Eastern Texts Relating to the Old Testament,* 2nd ed. Princeton, NJ: Princeton University Press, 1969.

Rawlinson, George. *Ancient Egypt,* 7th ed. New York: G. P. Putnam's Sons, 1893.

Redford, Donald B. *Akhenaten: The Heretic King.* Princeton, NJ: Princeton University Press, 1984.

Reed, Bika. *Rebel in the Soul.* New York: Inner Traditions, 1978.

———. *The Field of Transformations.* Rochester, VT: Inner Traditions, 1987.

Rossiter, Evelyn. *The Book of the Dead: Papyri of Ani, Hunefer, Anhai.* Geneva: Productions Liber SA, 1979.

Schwaller de Lubicz, Isha. *The Opening of the Way.* New York: Inner Traditions, 1981.

Schwaller de Lubicz, R. A. *The Egyptian Miracle.* New York: Inner Traditions, 1981.

———. *Nature Word.* West Stockbridge, MA: Lindisfarne, 1982.

———. *Symbol and the Symbolic.* Brookline, MA: Autumn Press, 1978.

———. *The Temple in Man.* Brookline, MA: Autumn Press, 1978.

Sewall, Barbara. *Egypt Under the Pharaohs.* New York: G. P. Putnam's Sons, 1968.

West, John Anthony. *Serpent in the Sky.* New York: Julian Press, 1987.

White, J. E. Manchip. *Ancient Egypt.* New York: Dover, 1970.

Wilson, John A. *The Burden of Egypt.* Chicago: University of Chicago Press, 1951.

About the Author

NORMANDI ELLIS is an award-winning author, ordained Spiritualist minister, and high priestess in the Fellowship of Isis. In 2020, she received her doctor of divinity in comparative religions. In addition to *Awakening Osiris*, she has published fifteen books of nonfiction, fiction, and poetry. Among these are *Dreams of Isis*, *Feasts of Light*, *Invoking the Scribe*, *Imagining the World into Existence*, and *The Union of Isis and Thoth*. Her most recent book is *The Ancient Tradition of Angels*.

Since 1991, she has been leading spiritual journeys to Egypt. Her travel company, TwoLadiesTravelco, makes sojourns twice a year. She splits her time between Camp Chesterfield in Anderson, Indiana, where she directs the metaphysical program, and her writing studio in Frankfort, Kentucky. She can be reached at *www.normandiellis.com* for classes in metaphysics, Egyptology, and creative writing, as well as clairvoyant and astrological consultations.